1001 Budget Tips

Carmel McCartin

1001 Budget Tips

Favourites from Budget Bitch.

Published 2013 by Budget Bitch Australia

Editing & Formatting: Michael Betts

Publisher: Budget Bitch Pty Ltd

ABN 65 123 977 480

Kingston Road Thurgoona NSW 2640

www.BudgetBitch.com.au

ISBN 978 0 9875113 0 0

CONTENTS

FOREWORD

Having a budget doesn't mean being a cheapskate. Nor does it mean you must live frugally.

It's about making the most of the money you have today.

This book holds a collection of just 1001 of my favourite Budget Tips. Some of them are old, some are new. Some of these tips have been passed down through my family, whilst others have been collected and collated from all over the world.

There are some tips that I've written for you and some that I've learned the hard way. All of them are useful.

There's no doubt that you will have heard or learned some of these Budget Tips before. Just reading them again will remind you of their worth.

It's not just a reference book though; I've included some pages for you to jot down the hints you find most memorable or the things you want to put into action immediately.

I hope you will find this book helpful in making it easier to manage your money.

Carmel McCartin

Lifestyle

Entertainment
Holidays & Travel
Camping
Health & Fitness
Fashion
Beauty
Being Romantic
Transport & Cars
Fuel

Notes

Entertainment

1. Don't use the shopping mall/centre as a form of entertainment. Window shopping will always make you dissatisfied and want to spend more money.

2. Instead of going to the cinema, save your money by staying at home and hiring a DVD instead.

3. Gym memberships average $20 a week, so unless you are a regular, it is usually not value for money.

4. Eating out two fewer times a month will save you heaps!

5. Picnics can be a great form of inexpensive entertainment - you only need a nice day, some sandwiches, drinks and maybe a ball to throw around.

6. Giving gifts from the heart, instead of the wallet can relieve a lot of stress during holidays and special occasions.

7. Go to the library to borrow your books, rather than buy them.

8. Rent toys instead of buying them - or join a toy library.

9. Check out the local museums - most of them are free and have organised children's activities during the school holidays.

10. At your local cinema, check out which day of the week is the day they have discounted tickets.

11. Get creative! Plan to make all the gifts for Christmas this year. You may need to start early if your list is large.

12. A luxuries night out does not have to be expensive. Skip the appetizer, order wine by the glass and drink more water, then share a great dessert. Keep an eye out for happy hour specials and see the latest weekend matinee.

13. Instead of hitting the spa for a full-on day, take advantage of seasonal packages or just go for a soak in the hot tub.

14. Splurge once in a while - the key to living on a small budget is to focus on your financial goals first and then splurge on your luxury items afterward.

15. Join a babysitting club - that way everybody gets to share the load at inexpensive prices. And if you can't find one - start one!

16. Have a picnic on the couch - complete with wine and cheese.

17. Look online for special offers from theme parks. Often they have a discount if you print the page and take it when you buy tickets.

18. If you belong to a large extended family, gift giving at Christmas can be costly. Consider having a 'Kris Kringle'.

19. Board games are a great investment and properly cared for can last a long time. I still have my grandmother's edition of Scrabble and the entertainment value hasn't diminished or cost anything!

20. If you're a senior, don't leave home without your Seniors Card. It entitles you to discounts at shops, cafes, restaurants and cinemas displaying the Seniors Card sign.

21. Free is good! Listen to the radio instead of buying CDs, watch Free-To-Air TV instead of Pay TV, go to the library, and walk in the park.

22. Check papers, notice boards, websites specially designed with offers of cheap or unwanted tickets to concerts, sports events etc.

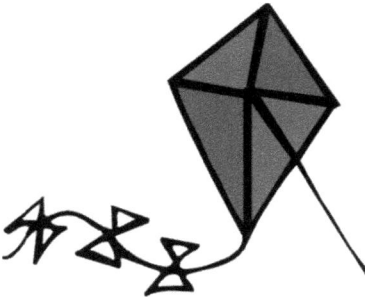

23. Kite flying is great on a windy day. You can make them yourself and save even more money.

24. Download free audio books for travelling with your kids, or just as something to use for 'quiet time'.

25. Print out free colouring pages off the internet instead of buying colouring books.

26. Organise a 'hand-me-down' party with your friends, and set a theme – kids clothes, kids toys, household goods etc.

27. Set up an obstacle course in your home (pillows, chairs, toys etc.) and have fun at home rather than taking the kids to a play centre.

28. Zoos are also fairly cheap and offer entertainment for the entire family.

29. Outdoor concerts - councils are always running free outdoor concerts in local parks. Keep an eye on your local newspaper to see what's coming up in your neighbourhood.

30. Go to the beach - one of the most wonderfully entertaining places in the world is absolutely free.

31. Plan a meal, invite your friends over and ask them to not only bring some of the ingredients, but tell them that they can help with the cooking. It's a very social activity.

32. Learn a new skill - many activities have free instructions or lessons via the internet. Just do a search for the ones that interest you and you're on your way!

33. Some art galleries have open-to-the-public exhibits that have no entry fees. You'll meet like-minded people and spend some time surrounded by culture.

34.   Jigsaw puzzles are an inexpensive source of many hours of entertainment. You can buy them for only a few dollars at your local thrift shop because many people use them once, and then get rid of them.

35.   Take your camera and go on a 'photo expedition'. Pick one subject for the day (all the trees in a particular park, a certain type of bird, shells on a beach, cars at the shopping centre, certain coloured cars etc.) and then get a group together to see who can find the most first.

36.   Look for opportunities to volunteer in your community. It can be official and organised such as in a homeless shelter or nursing home, or it could be spontaneous and organised by you - mowing lawns, cleaning parks, or babysitting for a single mother.

37.   Papier-mâchè is a great way to entertain the kids on a wet day. Have plenty of old newspapers on hand and make your own glue from a recipe of flour and water. They'll love making the piñata for Christmas, or their very own piggy bank. You're only limited by your imagination.

38.   Categorise your CDs, DVDs, or books into alphabetical order. This might sound boring, but you'll re-discover things you forgot you had and you'll also rediscover the enjoyment.

39.   Organise and spend a night of 'camping out' in your living room. The kids will love you for it!

40. Write an adventure story with your kids - then get it printed out and bind it in a cheap display binder. Make copies for the grandparents as a Christmas or birthday present.

41. Download and assemble free paper games/models from the internet.

42. Pull out your roller-blades or your bike, and call a friend to join you.

43. It's cheaper to buy ex-rental DVDs than it is to rent them.

44. If you want to eat at an expensive restaurant, go for lunch rather than dinner. The menu is usually the same, but the prices are often half.

45. Make the most of any available student discounts. Show your child's school ID at museums, zoos, galleries, theatres, etc.

46. Rather than buying separate admissions to different educational or fun family destinations, buy one yearly family pass to the zoo, the aquarium, or a theme park. Go

repeatedly to that one place each time you want a family outing. You will easily save the cost of the family admission, plus you'll have the benefit of not feeling pressured to see everything in one day. And, believe me - you won't get bored as these places are constantly changing things to keep you entertained.

47.   Always, take your own food & drinks when visiting theme parks, the zoo, or anywhere there is an admission fee. This will help to keep the cost of an outing to a minimum.

48.   Be patient and wait to see new movies on DVD. Some public libraries offer free DVD rentals and will order new movies if library patrons request a certain title.

49.   Find a local berry farm, and pick your own berries.

50.   Find a local orchard and pick your own fruit.

Things to Do

Holidays and Travel

1. Airfares are cheaper if you buy in advance and if you book online.

2. Flying midweek is also cheaper than weekend travel.

3. You could save hundreds of dollars by holidaying during low or shoulder travel seasons.

4. Being flexible about trip dates and times makes a difference in fare prices.

5. Setup automatic bill payments while you're away to avoid late fees.

6. When flying with a family choose a discount airline to save money.

7. Book your airline flights well in advance because as your holiday draws closer, cheaper departure dates and times may no longer be available.

8. Travel light – most airlines are now charging for luggage. If you can carry everything in a small suitcase you'll save money.

9. Make sure you don't get charged for 'excess baggage'.

10. If you're able to get them – a rail pass is a much cheaper option than buying several point to point tickets.

11. The cheapest travel option of all is to walk once you reach your destination. Tour the town by foot and you will get a fascinating and a healthy view of the sites.

12. Low season hotel rates are very affordable so try to plan your holidays around these times.

13. Flights that depart early in the morning or late at night are often the cheapest.

14. Bed and Breakfast places also have excellent last minute rates; especially in the low season when they are more interested in filling their rooms than pulling in a huge profit.

15. A good alternative to hotels is hostels. They're not just for the young backpackers, and can save you lots of dollars.

16. Camping is another inexpensive option.

17. If you need a place to stay, you may save money by getting a package deal which includes airfares and accommodation.

18. Rather than eating out three meals a day, pack a cooler and stock up on treats for the trip. You can have a quiet picnic

along the way and will not have to fork out snack money at every fuel stop.

19. If you're staying at a hotel, take advantage of complimentary continental breakfasts.

20. Holiday insurance is a good idea, but it's important to know exactly what you're covered for.

21. Finding 'Kids Eat Free!' offers or discounts on certain meals will ease the holiday budget.

22. If you plan to stay in a city a long time, renting an apartment can be a good option. Furnished apartments are usually cheaper than hotels and, you'll get the comforts of home without spending a lot of money.

23. If you're driving - watch the speed limits. A great holiday can become a financial disaster if you end up having to pay speeding fines.

24. Think small when renting a car. A compact or standard size vehicle will cost less than a minivan or SUV (and will save on fuel).

25. Check the local online newspaper of the place you are visiting and search for special money saving coupons, discounts and any special offers that you can find to take advantage of.

26. Consider distance. If your budget is extremely tight, determine how far you can travel and how long you can be away.

27. If you're planning to go overseas, pick a location with a good exchange rate. Or choose a spot where there are lots of free activities.

28. Keep it close and short. Day trips are cheaper than overnight or multi-day trips. If you're flying or taking the train you may want to stay longer to get your money's worth.

29. Bike rather than drive or fly. Who says a car or flight is the only way to go? Biking is great fun, good exercise and is better for the environment. Most reasonably fit people can cycle at least 20 - 30 kms in one day.

30. Walking tours (literally called 'Free Tours') are the cheapest way to enjoy a guided tour of any town/region.

31. Consider a working holiday and seek out opportunities that combine work and travel.

32. Consider a 'house-swap' in a different part of the country, or even in a different country. You can find more information about this online.

33. Keep your eye open for special air fare deals, especially when a new company enters the marketplace.

34. Enter into bidding on TV holiday auctions, as long as you are prepared to pay what you bid. You can get some great deals.

35. Shop around for the best place to change foreign cash and traveller's cheques. Look for money exchange places in the cities where competition between banks and foreign exchange outlets mean that you'll get a better deal.

36. Register with an Australian House Sitters site. It's a great way to save money on accommodation and see many parts of Australia at the same time.

37. You can save money on car rental if the car rental companies have vehicles that need to be relocated. It doesn't hurt to enquire!

38. Weigh your suitcase on the bathroom scales before you leave home to make sure you don't get hit for excess baggage charges when checking in for your flight.

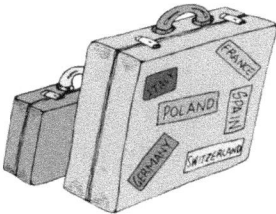

39. Avoid exchanging money at the airport, money exchange offices at airports are known for additional fees.

40. Have a few alternative funds sources such as credit/debit cards, travellers' cheques and overseas currency.

41. Take a pocket record of exchange rates so you can compare to the Aussie dollar and know what your dollar is buying.

42. Cities often give tourist info away for free, and you'd be amazed at what you don't know about your hometown that tourists do, because you've never taken the time to explore.

43. Act like a tourist, look around, and I bet you'll learn things that you didn't even know you didn't know!

44. When you're on the road it's so tempting to eat out at restaurants every night. Why not go for lunch instead? Lunch menus are usually much cheaper than evening menu's for dinner.

45. Be aware of local customs. E.g. throughout Italy, there are often two separate prices for the same cup of coffee; one if you stand at the bar with the locals - and another (more exorbitant) price if you sit at a table and have a waiter serve you.

46. Eat what the locals eat - and where they eat. A good tip is to wander away from the main tourist areas for your evening meal.

47. Head for the food courts in any of the shopping malls at around closing time and grab dinner for a fraction of the cost.

48. Australia is full of great wine regions, and while purchasing wines will obviously cost money, sampling them usually won't. Do it even cheaper and cycle from vineyard to vineyard.

49. Refill your water bottle at a public bubbler (water fountain) instead of spending $2.50 per bottle of water.

50. Take advantage of 'shopper dockets' and coupons, which have meal and drink offers on the reverse of receipts issued with purchases.

51. While overseas divert your mobile calls to voicemail and just use SMS to communicate – so much cheaper.

52. Make copies of your passport, credit cards and other travel documents and keep them separate in your luggage. Also leave copies at home with family. Having to replace these items whilst on holiday is very expensive and time consuming.

53. If you're staying in hostels watch out for cheap meals on offer. Or you can help with cooking meals for a greatly reduced price (or even free).

54. Don't drive for hours and hours without having a break. Stop, Revive & Survive stations offer free tea + coffee.

55. If you're in a vehicle, watch where you park. Nothing eats into a travel budget faster than parking tickets.

56. Check your email; make travel arrangements etc. from your smart phone or laptop from free Wi-Fi hotspots. Find and use the internet using free Wi-Fi at popular coffee shops and the golden arches.

57. Instead of spending lots of money going away on holidays why not stay at the 'Just Like Home Motel' (your place) and visit all the tourist attractions around your own area! Other people pay big money to visit these places while you have them right at your doorstep! You can go on the day tours etc. and 'act like a tourist'! You will save lots of money and maybe discover places you never knew about before!

58. If money is too tight for resorts and you don't fancy camping then check out the on-site vans and cabins in caravan parks.

59. Try to use ATMs during business hours at a bank. That way, if your card disappears, you'll be able to have it retrieved much easier.

60. Make an effort to learn some of the local language. You'll be less likely to be ripped off! Also - a few smiles and a bit of effort can go a long way to securing you a great bargain.

Camping

1. Lots of items that you need to take camping can be found at home or bought at the supermarket: pots and pans, cups and glasses, cutlery, pillows, torches, extra batteries, and food.

2. It's cheaper to shop online for your other camping gear, or go to one of the large department stores; they have most of what you'll need at the lowest prices.

3. Buy a cheap tarp for around $10. This will have many uses – under or over the tent, as a wind shield outside, around 4 poles for use as a semi-permanent shower or dunny. Your imagination is your limit here.

4. Food and drinks can be kept cool in a cooler/esky/ portable fridge. Keep the ice in their bags, and open the lid as few times as possible. This will keep the cool air in, which will keep the ice frozen longer.

5. Inexpensive long-life milk will keep better and longer (if unopened). Buy a good supply before you leave - at the lowest price you can find.

6. If you're travelling in the outback, don't expect fresh bread everywhere. Freeze some before you go, and use stale bread for toast.

7. Take your meat supply with you - frozen. Always use the cuts that have a bone in them first (chops etc.) as the bone does not freeze well, and this is the first meat-cut to deteriorate.

8. Pre-cook and freeze some meals – e.g. lasagne, casseroles, and pasta dishes. Packed with ice, in a cooler, they will last more than a few days and will save time, money and decision making.

9. Take large containers with your home water supply. This will save you many dollars.

10. After showering, wipe yourself with a 'chux' cloth (or similar) to remove excess water. Then dry off with your towel. Doing this will mean that your towels are fresher for longer, before you need to launder them.

Health and Fitness

1. The one essential ingredient for fitness, healthy living, or weight loss that costs nothing is determination. You can't buy it, but you can find it inside you.

2. Don't pay expensive gym fees - put on your shoes and go for a walk!

3. Before you join a gym, take a trial membership to make sure you like going and will continue with the program.

4. Replace sugary drinks with water. (Tap water is the cheapest option if your local supply is palatable).

5. If you have a cleaning lady, get rid of her. Cleaning your house isn't work; it's exercise. Get out your cleaning supplies and scrub/vacuum your way to a trimmer you.

6. Need to do a cardio-workout? Get an inexpensive rope and have a skipping session.

7. Mowing the lawn, weeding the garden, raking the leaves or shoveling are all low cost ways to exercise.

8. Take a healthy lunch to work - saves calories and money!

9. Always put leftovers into the fridge for tomorrow. Do not eat them!

10. Replace store bought snacks with fresh fruit.

11. Reducing the size of your food portions will save calories and also save money on the grocery bill.

12. Remove temptation for chocolate bars by only going to the supermarket once a week.

13. Look in your pantry - many canned goods can serve double duty as hand weights.

14. If you have a sedentary job, make sure you get up from your desk and exercise for 5 minutes every hour. At the end of an 8 hour day, you will have done 40 minutes of exercise.

15. Walking to work will burn calories and save money on petrol and car running expenses.

16. Turn on some music and dance. It's great exercise and costs very little money.

17. Always remember that the object is to reduce your body size - not your wallet.

18. Avoid costly commercialised diet plans.

19. Planning your meals in advance is not only good for your waistline, but also your wallet.

20. Rent large personal gym equipment items instead of buying them. It's cheaper to 'hire and use' than it is to 'purchase and store away'.

21. After 6 months of renting and using gym equipment, ask the store if you could purchase the item – at a reduced price of course. (It's now 'used' isn't it?)

22. Borrow exercise DVDs from your library rather than buying them.

23. Get a regular 7 to 8 hours of sleep every night. When you're tired you get grumpy and start eating costly unhealthy food to cheer you up.

24. Buy a 'pool pass' if swimming is part of your exercise regime. It will be much cheaper than 'pay as you swim' if you're doing it regularly.

25. Snack smarter by taking your own snack from home rather than hitting the vending machines. It's much more expensive to buy individual snacks from the machines than to portion out servings from full-size packages into zipper bags.

26. You can buy a six-pack of diet soft drink for the same cost that you'll purchase two or three from a vending machine.

27. Find your nearest tennis court where you can play for free.

28.	Beans are cheap to buy, high in fibre and low in fat. You can feed your family a hearty filling meal for just a few dollars.

29.	Drink a glass of water when you feel hungry. Many times what you mistake for hunger is actually thirst.

30.	Some sporting goods stores specialise in used equipment. Search listings for exercise equipment in either the local newspaper or online.

31.	Resistance bands are cheap, portable, and can be used to work out almost every muscle in your body. Most of them come with a set of instructions.

32.	You don't need expensive shakes and pre-packaged meals or the latest piece of exercise equipment to lose weight. Get your mind right about this and your body will follow suit.

33.	You can shed kilos on a budget simply by eating fewer calories and burning more calories.

34.	If you really do want to join a gym, look for one that will allow you to take out a monthly membership. That way you can stop without wasting money if you can't continue.

35.	Brush your teeth if you feel tempted by snacking - it takes away the urge to eat.

36.	You don't need expensive exercise clothing to exercise. Save your money for buying new clothing that will fit your trimmer and tauter body.

37. Eat at home more. You can't be tempted by a dessert menu at home!

38. Don't buy diet pills. Diet pills work for one group of people only; the people selling them.

39. Eating slowly is a good weight-loss strategy, and making food spicier is an easy way to do it.

40. With bike paths and tracks in most cities these days, it's very safe to ride your bike as an inexpensive way to exercise.

Starting tomorrow,
I'm going to ….

Fashion

1. Sort out your wardrobe, to make sure you're only buying what you need and what you don't already have.

2. Fix and alter what you have first rather than spending money on new.

3. Before purchasing new clothing use the rule of three:
    - Do you have 3 things that go with this item?
    - Do you have 3 places to wear it?
    - Do you have 3 different ways to accessorise it?

4. Always shop off-season, on weekdays and at sale time.

5. Don't shop without a list. It's like food shopping when you're hungry!

6. Have clothes like basic jeans, cardigans and blazers as they can be worn anytime and anywhere no matter what the season.

7. When buying essential clothing like jeans etc. - buy basic colours. They can always be fashioned-up with new season's coloured accessories.

8. Remember this - the more well known the brand name, the bigger the price.

9. Changing the buttons on a garment will give it a new and higher quality appearance.

10. Unless you're constantly undressing in public - underwear does not need to be brand named. Many of the cheaper brands are better value.

11. Accessories are an easy and inexpensive way to get an updated look.

12. Mix all different styles and eras together to get a custom look.

13. Trendy items always become dated quickly. Just buy one or two pieces every season and mix them in with your wardrobe staples like the little black dress or basic denim jeans.

14. Adding a scarf will change the look of an outfit without costing much money.

15. Shops have a much better selection on weekdays because the stores don't have time to restock on weekends.

16. Move out of your shopping comfort zone and venture into cheaper stores you usually wouldn't think to go in; vintage shops, charity shops and flea markets. You just never know where you'll find the best bargain fashion looks.

17. Think quality, not quantity. Buy the best you can afford and wear it for years and years, rather than buy a load of really cheap clothes that won't last a month.

18. You must try on every article of clothing that you want to buy. Impulse buying is a bad habit that often results in a

regretful purchase of ill-fitting, ugly clothes you simply don't want once you get home.

19. If you have a friend/relative who is the same size and has similar taste then don't be afraid to share. You'll have twice as many outfits to choose from.

20. When you don't have the money to shop for clothing all the time, you can create fresh looks with what you already have in your wardrobe by wearing things in new and different ways.

21. Learn to sew – and create your own style for half the price.

22. When shopping for trendy items; try to find things that you can wear with multiple outfits in your closet.

23. If you really don't want anybody to know that your clothing is not from designer boutiques - cut the tags off.

24. Fresh nail polish and clean shoes will give extra sparkle to your appearance. (And they don't cost much!)

25. Keep all receipts and tags and if you haven't worn a garment within two weeks of purchase; take it back.

26. Don't forget to check out factory outlets - many times you'll find the exact item you're searching for, at a heavily discounted price.

27. Check the care labels on each garment. If your money is tight, you may find it difficult to afford a weekly dry-cleaning bill.

28. Good foundation garments will make your outfit look sensational - no matter what you're wearing.

29. Jewellery adds focus and a focal point for your outfit. Costume jewellery is an inexpensive way of changing the look of a garment.

30. A summer sarong/pareo has a multitude of uses and there are many ways they can be worn.

Beauty

1. You don't need to pay for fancy packaging and a popular brand name - most shampoos, shower gels and facial cleansers have got identical ingredients in them (read the labels on the back).

2. For an inexpensive face firming mask, just open the fridge and crack open an egg. Apply the whites to the skin and let it sit for about 10 minutes.

3. White sugar is the cheapest & sweetest exfoliator around. Lather up your face and body in the shower, and use a handful of white sugar to scrub away any dead skin cells.

4. Head to the Beauty School or College – students are always looking for models to practise their skills. The cost is very reasonable, and the rookies are heavily supervised.

5. Home colouring kits have come a long way in both ease of use and safety for your hair. Ask your friends for recommendations to find the right brand for you.

6. Check out the makeup counters in large department stores and find one that offers a free facial.

7. Olive oil can be added to bath water for a skin softener.

8. Cut back on the amount of shampoo you use. Do the same with toothpaste. The manufacturers want us to use more so that we buy more but they both end up down the drain.

9.   Rinsing your hair with cider apple vinegar really does leave it silky and shiny.

10.   Witch hazel is a great toner for oily skin as well as being useful for cleansing cuts and grazes. You can buy it cheaply in all good chemists/pharmacies.

11.   Use soap or hair conditioner instead of expensive shaving foam.

12.   Buy a decent base coat and top coat, and use cheap nail varnish in between the layers.

13.   Look for a home hairdresser and you'll find the prices are cheaper than in the salons.

14.   A cheap remedy for tired eyes - haemorrhoid cream will also reduce the bags under your eyes. (Only use if you have this on hand. Don't buy the cream unless you have haemorrhoids).

15.   Vaseline is good for dry skin, particularly on knees and elbows. Vaseline is economical to buy.

16.   Learn to give yourself a manicure. For the price of one manicure, you can buy a kit that will last you several months.

17.   Out of shampoo? Try a herbal tea rinse.

18.   Toothpaste on facial spots and insect bites will help to eliminate them.

19. Cucumber slices will reduce puffy eyes. (They're not just for salads).

20. Tea tree oil is good for pimples, ingrown hairs and as a disinfectant. It costs a lot less than other expensive cures.

21. Keep your nail varnish in the fridge to make it last longer.

22. Lemon juice can whiten the tips of your nails.

23. Store makeup pencils in the fridge so they do not crumble when you sharpen them. When they last longer, you spend less on them.

24. Hair removal cream will also remove fake tan.

25. Coffee grounds are good as a body scrub to help remove cellulite.

26. Use a little lipstick on your cheeks if you have run out of blusher. Applying a dab of lip gloss to your cheeks will give you a dewy, healthy glow.

27. Use olive oil as a hair and hand conditioner. A little bit goes a long way.

28. Use baby wipes to remove your make-up. They're cheaper!

29. If your mascara has dried out too quickly, simply run it under hot water for five minutes to reliquify it.

30. If you have a bunch of half used lipsticks, scoop them out of their tubes. You can mix and blend up new colours to create your own professional lipstick palette. Add a little Vaseline in the mix, and you will have a tinted gloss.

31. When using moisturiser, apply any excess on to the backs of your hands and elbows to make sure none is wasted.

32. Mix lipsticks with lip balm, and they'll last longer.

33. Rub half a lemon under your arms as a natural deodorant.

34. Always use a moisturiser with built-in sunscreen rather than layering sunscreen and moisturiser which can clog pores.

35. Milk is rich in protein and fat, both of which calm irritated skin. Add two to four cups of whole milk to a warm bath and have a soak.

36. Before applying lipstick or gloss, simply rub a bit of moistened cinnamon on your lips or a drop of cinnamon oil to get plumper/fuller lips without all the chemicals and the hefty price tag!

37. If you're fair-skinned, baby powder/talc can be dusted on as a foundation setting powder.

38. Use olive oil to remove your makeup; it's fabulous for quickly removing stubborn eyeliner.

39. If you can't afford perfume; try out some body-sprays. They're cheap and cheerful.

40. Sprinkle some baking soda on a damp toothbrush and brush as normal. You'll have whiter teeth without the investment in expensive whiteners.

41. Rose water is the most effective and inexpensive toner for your skin.

42. Vaseline is the most inexpensive cuticle butter. Just use it on your cuticles daily before going to bed.

43. Store your make-up and fragrance in a cool, dark place to extend their life span.

44. Add your favourite eau de toilette to some olive oil and use as scented bath oil.

45. A drop of water to the remains of a foundation will make sure you use every last drop.

46. Forget about buying eyeliner. With a small, angled brush and a little water, your eye-shadow colours can work as eyeliner.

Reminders

Being Romantic

1. Write a poem about the one you love and share it with them.

2. Cook dinner and serve in a romantic setting (you know - candles, flowers, soft lighting).

3. Give each other a full-body massage.

4. Pack a sunset picnic and enjoy each other's company as the sun goes down. You can do this anywhere!

5. Pick wildflowers on the way home. (Please, not in the National Park).

6. Burn a CD with love songs and listen together.

7. Give chocolates often. Don't wait for special occasions.

8. Read poetry together. (Out loud, preferably).

9. Prepare a special dessert of strawberries with fondue chocolate; the food of love.

10. Snuggle together on a rainy day.

11. Leave little love notes everywhere. Putting one in the middle of the lunchtime sandwich will definitely get a reaction.

12. Send a love email every day.

13. Take a moonlit walk on the beach.

14. Snuggle together on the couch while watching romantic movies.

15. Get some good wine; watch shooting stars.

16. Take a bath together (use bubbles).

17. Bring home good coffee or a decadent sweet and share!

18. Take a walk down memory lane - visit some of the special places from your early days of dating.

19. Make a special cake; decorate it with a love message.

20. Make a scrapbook with photos, mementos and little notes from your lives together.

21. Kiss in the rain. (It might be wet, but it's also very romantic).

22. Ride a Ferris Wheel together; hold hands. If you don't like heights, burrow your head into your partners shoulder.

23. Sneak away from a party and make out.

24. Bring home great take-away and light some candles.

25. Do something special that you know will make your partner happy.

26. Slow dance to romantic music.

27. Take an afternoon nap together.

28. Kiss slowly; touching his or her back and neck and nape with the tips of your fingers - slowly.

29. Make a list of everything you love about him or her. Share it with each other.

30. Write a love letter. Make sure your partner gets to read it.

31. Clip or email things that make you think of your partner, every day.

32. Go to a movie; ignore the movie and make out like teenagers.

33. Take extra care to groom yourself, so as to look extra good for your partner. They do appreciate it.

34. Take some quiet time together and talk about your day.

35. Go parking. How long is it since you did that?

36. Feed each other grapes. If you find that boring, then do it blindfolded.

37. Recreate your partner's favourite romantic movie scene.

38. Pretend you're going on a first date - show up at the door with flowers, all dressed up, with your car washed and cleaned, looking spiffy. Recreate the first time.

39. Create a little box with a bunch of your partner's favourite things inside.

40. Paint each other with flavoured body paint. Be creative!

41. Try some sexy role-playing. Get dressed up, be daring, have fun.

42. Give a little token to your partner to wear and say it's to remind him or her all day that you love them.

43. Sing a favourite song to him or her. Only do this if you can sing in tune.

44. Have dinner on the roof, with some candles. Warning! This doesn't work if your roof slopes sharply.

45. Hold hands and walk somewhere with lots of pretty lights.

46. Say I love you in a different way, every day.

47. Blindfold your partner. Use a feather. Slowly.

48. Declare your love very publicly. (Get down on one knee in public; that sort of thing).

49. Send a gift through the mail to your partner's workplace.

50. Phone your partner - just to say I love you.

Things to Change

Transport and Cars

1.   If you have to drive to work and you live near other work colleagues, arrange to car-pool and share the petrol and parking costs with your friends.

2.   Check the tyre pressure on your car at least once a month to ensure your tyres are properly inflated. This can improve the fuel efficiency of your car and extend the life of your tyres.

3.   If you have a small chip on your car windscreen, try to get it fixed as soon as possible. Fixing an entire windscreen will cost much more than fixing a minor chip.

4.   If you feel comfortable riding a bike, why not invest in a scooter. It's much cheaper to run than a car and parking in the city is a breeze!

5.   Do you really need two cars? Or even one? Or could you make do with a cheaper car?

6.   Use standby air fares if it's not really urgent when you fly.

7. Learn how to service your own vehicles. Adult education courses can teach you the basics of changing the oil and lubricating what needs to be lubricated.

8. Haggle over the price of a new car. Once the dealer has given you the price, ask - is that the best price you can offer me? You may have to repeat this up to 5 times before you get the rock-bottom price.

9. Don't pay for the extended warranty on your new car. Consumer reports are saying that they're a waste of money.

10. Downsize your car and save money, not only in monthly payments but also in maintenance, insurance and operating expenses.

11. Rotate your tyres to the manufacturer's recommendation - this will ensure all tyres wear evenly and will provide a longer life as well.

12. If you use public transport every day - buy a periodical ticket (weekly, monthly, yearly).

13. If you buy a yearly ticket, make sure that you use it every day.

14. If you ring your car insurance provider right now and request to increase your voluntary excess you should get an immediate refund of what you have over paid. But make sure that you can handle the higher voluntary excess.

15. Check your air filter. A dirty air filter restricts the flow of air into the engine, which harms performance and economy.

16. One of the best ways to save fuel is to simply reduce your speed. As speed increases, fuel economy decreases exponentially.

17. Avoid heavy traffic and lots of traffic lights. The shortest route is not always the most fuel efficient if you have to stop a lot.

18. Try to combine trips for car travel. If you live outside of town, try to go into town only once and get everything you need done at the one time.

19. Don't wait until the fuel tank is empty before you buy petrol. If you do, you will find yourself at the mercy of service station pricing policies. Fill up more often so you can buy at the best price.

20. If you live within walking distance of your local shopping venue, walk there and back, and arrange to have your weekly groceries delivered by the store.

21. You can improve your fuel economy by up to 2% by using the proper grade of motor oil.

22. Keep it capped! Did you know about 556 million litres of petrol evaporate every year from vehicles without petrol caps?

23. Keeping up with regular vehicle maintenance can allow you to increase your fuel economy by an average of 4%.

24. Your car will also be more energy efficient if the wheel alignment is correctly set and the brakes aren't dragging.

25. A cold engine is less fuel-efficient and emits more pollutants than a warm engine; so several shorter trips will use more fuel than one longer trip.

26. If you don't always use or need a car, consider 'borrowing' one when you need it. There are a number of 'car sharing' companies that have been established for this purpose, such as Go Get, Flexicar etc.

27. Avoid paying parking fees by searching for free timed spaces. These can usually be found only a block or two beyond the paid parking areas. The extra exercise walking will do you good also.

28. Wash your car at home on the lawn and it will be a win-win for both the lawn and your pocket.

29. Shop around for servicing and mechanical quotes. Having your vehicle serviced by the manufacturer is generally not the cheapest and many workshops/garages can provide servicing that does not void the manufacturer's warranty.

30. If you want to buy a new car, consider purchasing a demo model. It will be less expensive than a new car but will still provide all the latest features as well as the new car warranty.

31. Shop around for Green-slip insurance. Prices vary depending on the town the car will be garaged, the ages of the driver(s) etc. A good comparison site can be found on the internet.

32. Join a motoring organisation which offers breakdown service plus other benefits/discounts.

33. Ensure you use the correct additives for your radiator coolant. These will not only prolong the life of your radiator but will also make your vehicle run more efficiently.

34. Have a regular air-conditioner service undertaken on your car. There's nothing worse than the air-conditioner packing it in on the hottest day of the year.

Memo

Fuel

1. Fill up first thing in the morning when it's still cool.

2. Maintain the correct tyre pressure for your car.

3. Don't be a hot-head! Drive smoothly and avoid unnecessary acceleration. Aggressive acceleration can reduce your fuel economy by up to a whopping 33%!

4. Avoid using air-conditioning whenever possible.

5. Don't drive with open windows when travelling at high speeds. Open windows on the highway can reduce fuel efficiency by 10%.

6. If you don't use your car roof racks often, remove them and other items which make your car less aerodynamic when they're not being used. Leaving them on only makes your car less fuel efficient and costs you money.

7. Even on cold mornings, cars don't need to idle more than 30 seconds. Newer cars are designed to be driven almost immediately and letting your car idle longer is a waste of petrol.

8. Remove any unnecessary items from the boot or the back seat of your car. These all add weight and can reduce the fuel efficiency of your car. Many people use their car boot as a storage space adding unneeded kilos to the car's weight.

This additional weight reduces the car's fuel efficiency by about 2% for every 50kg.

9. Cut down use. Plan your trips. You'll save time and fuel. Plan your car trip ahead of time to ensure you take the most direct route and avoid any possible traffic delays at peak hour traffic times. Also plan it so that you're doing a number of things in one go.

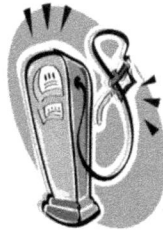

10. Service your car regularly. Keeping your vehicle well-tuned will reduce greenhouse gases by up to 5%. Having your car well maintained will help with the resale value.

11. Use discount fuel coupons that you get on supermarket dockets (or their loyalty cards) but don't drive miles out of your way just to get a bargain. The fuel for the trip may cost you more than you save!

In the Home

Around the House
Pet Care
Shopping
Baking
Sewing
Storage
Phone
In the Garden

Around the House

1. If your home has little or no ceiling insulation, it will pay to get some installed. You can save significant dollars on annual heating and cooling bills!

2. Finish your dishwasher cycle before the drying cycle and leave the door open to dry dishes.

3. Use off-peak energy and try to run electrical appliances during off-peak times e.g. run the pool pump overnight or use dishwashers and clothes-dryers during off-peak times.

4. Fridges account for a large portion of household energy because they run 24 hours a day. Ensure they are running efficiently by not opening the door too often and keeping them well filled.

5. Skip take-away, cook at home instead.

6. Thaw frozen foods fully before cooking. A little thought and preparation beforehand will help your money go further.

7. Generic medicines can save you hundreds of dollars per year. If you're not sure about the ingredients, ask your chemist.

8. Sell stuff you don't need on eBay or hold a garage sale. Reducing your hoarding habit will give you some extra cash.

9.   Because babies grow quickly, either buy their clothes at op shops or join forces with family and friends to share 'hand-me downs'.

10. Sponge clean your suit then hang it in the bathroom while you're showering to allow the steam to get rid of any creases.

11. With shirts and blouses, dab the backs of buttons with some clear nail polish to stop the thread unravelling. You won't have to waste money on repairs.

12. Grow your own fruit, herbs and vegetables. Do it on your patio if you haven't got a garden. Grow them hydroponically inside, if you don't have an outdoor area.

13. Share the cost of a mini skip with your neighbours and have a 'local' clean-up.

14. Make a list of all annual maintenance items for your home such as the air-conditioner, heater, hot water service, etc. Include appliances such as the lawn mower, barbecue, and so on. Being prepared and working in a proactive manner can save you unnecessary expenses.

15. Take cuttings from your garden, strike them in small pots and once established, use them for Christmas/birthday presents.

16. Make your own cleaning products from vinegar and bicarbonate of soda, instead of purchasing expensive commercial brands.

17. For a cheap window cleaner; one-part vinegar, three-parts water in a spray bottle.

18. If you own a pet dog, take it for a walk every day or night for a full fortnight to feel fit and healthy. It's cheaper than paying gym fees and your dog will also thank you for it!

19. Put on your shoes, and walk!

20. Take your lunch to work – you know this, you know how much you'll save each day – just do it! (Well, at least 3 times a week!)

21. When you are putting the groceries away into your pantry, bring the oldest cans and packets to the front and put the new ones at the back. This way you'll be using the oldest groceries first.

22. Take care of small repairs around your house, rather than hiring a handyman to do them.

23. Turn off lights when not needed, change to compact fluoro globes, rug up instead of having the heater on, cool down with a spray bottle.

24. Trade services – the old bartering system is a great way to save money. E.g. give a neighbour a haircut (if that's your

regular job) in return for a car service (if that's their regular job).

25. Save on family haircuts by learning how to do it yourself.

26. Install low flow tap aerators. They're not expensive and can save money on your water bill.

27. Turn your computer off when you're not using it. Computers drain a lot of power in standby mode.

28. Take care of your air-conditioner by performing basic maintenance yourself and getting a regular service call to tune it up. You'll lower the risk of something going wrong during the hot summer months when it will be more costly to repair.

29. Repair leaking taps – this will save water as well as keep the costs down on the water bill.

30. Make your own birthday and gift cards. The prices of these have increased dramatically and they often end up in the recycle bin anyway.

31. Use your children's art work as gift wrapping paper.

32. Wrap gifts in junk mail. It's brightly coloured and will probably end up in the same place as the expensive gift wrap.

33. Clean out filters - your air-conditioner and clothes dryer both build up a large amount of lint over a period of time. Cleaning them regularly will ensure that they run better, use less electricity and reduce the risk of fire.

34. Refill printer cartridges - these cost a bundle. Find somewhere that will refill your existing ones for you and save money.

35. Buy the cheapest brand of pasta, long-grained rice, sugar, flour - you will never notice the difference.

36. Outside awnings will reduce your cooling costs in summer and your heating costs in winter.

37. Window curtains will also help to keep the heat inside during winter.

38. Stay in touch with long distance friends and family by using Skype (Voice over Internet Protocol). In many instances – it's a free call.

39. Check gutters and downpipes for blockages, damage and rust. Repair/replace before they become a problem.

40. Regularly check security items around the home, including alarms, door & window locks, gates and fences.

Must Do

Pet Care

1. Feed your pet a homemade diet, it's definitely a cheaper option.

2. Form a co-op with pet-owning friends and share both the expense and the meal preparation work for homemade food.

3. Exercise with your pet – it will be good for both of you and help to keep the vet fees to a minimum.

4. Over feeding not only fattens your dog (which leads to expensive veterinary bills) but is also a waste of expensive dog food.

5. Brush your pet's teeth regularly – animal dental fees are rather costly.

6. Invest in some pet insurance or increase the amount of your emergency fund, because accidents do happen.

7. The cheapest way to groom your animal is to brush it regularly.

8. Buy a good quality grooming kit and clip your pet's coat regularly. Small dogs cost an average of $50 each time if you don't do this yourself. You'll recoup the money for the clippers very quickly.

9. Learn to trim your pet's toenails. This will also keep the grooming costs down.

10. Adopt a dog from an animal shelter. They've usually been desexed and have had all the injections appropriate for their age. If buying a puppy, these costs will be additional to the price of the dog.

11. If your dog likes stuffed toys, purchase them from thrift shops and garage sales. Take off any small buttons etc. that could choke your pet.

12. Although your dog is a valued member of your family, it is still an animal and doesn't need to wear human style clothing. Don't waste your money doing this.

13. Keep your eye out for low cost pet vaccination clinics which are often sponsored by local councils or animal shelters.

14. If you are hit by large unexpected vet bills, ask if you can have a payment plan.

15. Check out your local library for DVDs and books about animal training. Professional training is not cheap and you can learn to do it yourself, quite easily.

16. Holiday accommodation for pets is not cheap. Find another pet owner who is willing to care for your pet whilst you're away; in return for you reciprocating the favour.

17. Homemade pet treats are not only cost effective for you, but healthy for your pet.

18. Dog blankets can be expensive so look for inexpensive kids fleece blankets in department stores.

19. Wash your dog in your bath instead of buying another container for the purpose.

20. Not all vets charge the same amount. Shop around for the one that you can afford.

Checklist

Shopping

1. Don't go to the supermarket if you're hungry. It's guaranteed to give you a huge dose of 'impulse buying'.

2. Always take with you a list of what you definitely need at the supermarket.

3. If your local grocery store doesn't have unit pricing take a small calculator with you to work out the best deals.

4. Scanner errors at the checkout are very common, so you should know your prices and watch your items as they're being scanned.

5. When a supermarket sells out of advertised specials, ask for a rain check so you can buy that item at a low price when supplies are replenished.

6. Are you bargain hunting? The real bargains are on the top and bottom shelves. Make sure you check there first.

7. Save up to 70% by shopping at factory outlets.

8. Minimize the use of convenience foods - it's also a more healthy option to use fresh and unprocessed foods.

9. Don't use prepared mixes – making them yourself is cheaper and takes not much more effort than using prepared mixes.

10. Look for coupons for products you're buying. But don't buy products just because you have a coupon!

11. Plan menus for a week at a time, taking into account what foods are seasonably available and perhaps also 'on special' for the week.

12. Make your shopping list after you've planned your menu.

13. If you go to the supermarket near closing time there is usually marked down bakery products, maybe hot chickens and possibly meat or dairy items.

14. Eating meatless meals twice a week will keep your costs under control. There are lots of great vegetable recipes around these days.

15. Add legumes (e.g. beans and lentils) to your meat recipes to lower the cost and bulk out the meal at the same time.

16. Buy gifts to suit a person, not to a money value. Gifts thought out carefully and directed towards individual needs and interests are unique and more appreciated.

17. Keep a lookout for cheap/two for the price of one/free coupons.

18. Check out your local Op Shop - you'll be amazed at the prices there!

19. Save time and fuel by using the internet to compare prices, check guarantees, price policies, shipping costs and return policies.

20. Avoid shopping at the last minute by starting your Christmas shopping early. When under pressure, shoppers often buy more than what they need.

21. Fashionistas with limited budgets should follow the 70/30 rule: 70% of your closet should be classic pieces and 30% trendy pieces. Go as cheap as possible on trendy items because they have a shorter lifespan.

22. Learn where and when to buy - know when the best store sales are and where.

23. Decide what you are looking to buy. Don't just wander the shops waiting for inspiration. Decide before you go what it is that you will purchase.

24. Shop at the store that is the cheapest overall.

25. Buy next year's winter clothes at the end of the current season and save.

26. Comparison shopping is no longer a drawn out process – the internet has changed all that. Always do your research before making major purchases.

27. Food - buy larger (and less expensive) quantities. This will also save you fuel money by not running to the store as frequently.

28. Groceries - consider 'store brands' or generics. Check and compare the ingredients and nutritional information with the more expensive name brands. They are often nearly identical.

29. Don't be afraid to ask for a discount.

30. Be sure to check that a large packet of something is actually cheaper than several small packets. Sometimes the 'economy size' pack is more expensive per unit price!

31. Whenever possible, combine all your shopping into one day.

32. Where possible, buy in bulk.

33. Don't let others talk you into making a purchase that you can't afford and don't need.

34. Buying wholesale is always cheaper than buying at retail prices.

35. Stock up and freeze. Meat goods will store in the freezer for quite a long time, e.g. if you see mince on sale, buy a heap

of it, store it in a chest freezer and then use it as needed. It's better than buying a kilo here and a kilo there and spending a fortune.

36. Buy groceries at discount stores if you see them there at a better price than the supermarket.

37. Ask family members and or neighbours if they'd like to share with you by buying in bulk, e.g. 20kgs of washing powder is often cheaper per kg than buying smaller lots. Sharing the product and the cost will make it cheaper for everybody.

38. Don't be frightened of 'secondhand shops'. If it's good enough to donate your preloved goods, then surely it's good enough to shop there also.

39. Day old bread is often a lot cheaper in price; and if you have space in the freezer you won't be able to tell the difference after it's thawed.

40. Compare the prices between fresh and frozen vegetables. Sometimes the frozen variety can be a cheaper option as there is little waste.

41. Buy your chicken pieces from the deli section of the supermarket. They're cheaper than buying from the 'meat cabinet'.

42. Don't shop when you are hungry - you are likely to buy a lot more than you need.

43. Look at the cost of items by weight and compare for value for money. Unit pricing now makes this a lot easier in the supermarket.

44. Always look for the use by and best before date and make sure you will be able to use the product within this timeframe.

45. If food items are on special, think carefully as to whether you will use them before they become out of date. It is not a good deal if you don't use the product and it ends up in the bin.

46. Remember that chilled foods are perishable and have a limited shelf life. The convenience and economy of buying goods in large quantities is lost if the food deteriorates and spoils before you can use it, creating unnecessary food waste.

47. Internet shopping may be the easiest way to do your grocery shopping without impulse buying. But bear in mind that you may not be able to compare all products or read nutrition labels.

48. Join a food co-op to enjoy the benefits of bulk buying. If you can't find one - start one!

49. Collecting coupons from newspapers, magazines and websites is not being miserly it will save you money in your grocery bill in the long run.

50. Shop less often - this will save you time and petrol

51. Pay for your purchases only with the cash you have allocated for food shopping. That way you can't be tempted to buy more than you need.

52. Convert your weekly supermarket allocation into store gift cards. You won't be able to overspend.

53. Day old bread is great for making breadcrumbs and puddings. Don't waste it by throwing it out.

54. Always check the meat cabinet for items that are marked down because they are close to their use by date.

55. Don't be overly fussy about buying the same brand every time. Often the cheaper brands are made by the same company that makes the more expensive item and the product is identical. It's just the packaging and your attitude that makes the difference.

56. Shopping alone will stop impulse demands from your children or spouse. It's the extras you buy to keep them quiet that will blow your budget.

57. Don't buy toilet rolls because they're on sale – unless you need them. There is always a sale on toilet rolls somewhere.

58. Be wary of 2 for 1 deals. If the product is not something you buy and use regularly, you'll find it sitting in your pantry many months later.

Notes

Baking

1. Find recipes that let you use what's in the cupboard. That end-of-the-bag coconut, dried fruit or white chocolate chips purchased at an earlier time, or a box of high fibre cereal pushed to the back of the cupboard can find their way into cookies, bars, quick breads and muffins.

2. Buy fruits in season and bake seasonal dishes to keep your costs per dish low, unless it is for a particularly special occasion.

3. A bag of carrots need not go limp in the fridge. Shred and add to baked goods for colour, moistness and added goodness.

4. It may be cheaper buying food in bulk, but unless you have a plan to use it all, you're wasting your money and food.

5. Baking cocoa can give you the same chocolate hit for less money than baking chocolate. Substitute cocoa for chocolate in recipes for cookies, cakes, frostings and brownies.

6. When you bake a batch of biscuits, make double the recipe and freeze the dough.

7. Turn leftover French or Italian bread into tasty bread puddings.

8.	Try baking an extra tray of muffins, freeze them and use them as lunch box snacks.

9.	If you store away left overs, always date their best before or expiration date to maintain the quality and freshness in your baking.

10.	Don't buy more pantry supplies than what you can use in a month or two so as to maintain freshness and eliminate spoilage.

11.	Greaseproof lunch wrap can also double as baking paper for half the cost.

12.	Inexpensive generic brand cake mixes can be used in many ways - cupcakes, muffins, puddings and slices.

13.	Don't toss away over-ripe bananas. They can be easily frozen, skin and all, until you have time to make some banana bread, cake or muffins.

Sewing

1. Only buy patterns and home décor fabrics when they are on sale.

2. Keep a basic dress and basic suit pattern that will not go out of style too soon. Altering the pattern each season will save you having to buy new ones every year.

3. Home décor fabric can be quite expensive. Consider using bed sheets and tablecloths when they are on sale - it's a great way to get a lot of fabric at a reasonable price.

4. You can find cheap fabric at Thrift stores. Manufacturers often donate rolls of fabric at the end of the season - you just have to find the stores that are the recipients of this gift.

5. If you have space, save your remnants. There are countless ways to use these in various projects - you only have to search the internet.

6. Buy your 'trims and notions' at sale times. (Buttons, zippers, laces, etc.).

7. Don't buy fabric just because it's on sale. Buy only the fabric you need for a specific project or you'll just end up with loads of fabric that is out of date and not the right quantity if you ever want to use it.

8. Check out the remnant box in the fabric store - there are often some great pieces there for little cost. But again, only buy with a specific project in mind.

9. Tracing your paper patterns onto interfacing will keep them in better condition for longer.

10. Work out how much you can afford to spend before buying a sewing machine. There are always excellent second-hand machines available. Remember it's the skill level that makes the garment - not the machine.

Storage

1. Ordinary shoe-boxes work well in sock & lingerie drawers. Saves time fossicking through everything for a pair of tights.

2. Ice cube trays make excellent multi-purpose storage devices; allowing you to hold the tiniest trinkets, office supplies, and craft components in their place.

3. Beautiful bento boxes are ideal for holding jewellery.

4. It only takes 3 planks of wood and 6 bricks to make a quick and sturdy set of shelves.

5. Recycle old cakes tins for storing craft glues and garden sprays.

6. Don't throw out biscuit tins - use them in your office, the garden shed or the play room. They're sturdy and make great storage units.

7. Cup hooks are always useful for holding keys, clothes, cords and numerous other items. Put them on the inside of cupboard doors if you don't like the look of them.

8. Second-hand wardrobes make great storage places in the garden shed or the workshop.

9. Install sturdy hooks from the ceiling of your garage to hang/suspend items from. It's a cheap and useful way of storing unused sporting equipment.

10. Hanging shoe organisers are inexpensive and can be used in every room of the house for storing small items & keeping things tidy.

Phone

1. Prepaid mobile phones are generally cheaper than contracts or if you use your mobile a lot you should look at capped plans.

2. Make a habit of researching whether to switch your mobile phone plan every year or so, to make sure you are on the best rates and can reduce your mobile phone bill where possible.

3. Make calls from a landline when possible as it is a fraction of the price of using a mobile phone.

4. Rather than pay by phone, pay all your bills online through your internet connection as this will save money on your phone bill.

5. When choosing a home phone provider make sure you choose a plan that suits your needs.

6. Remember that the cheaper the line rental, the more expensive the call rates may be.

7. Don't choose any phone plan (mobile or fixed line) that locks you into a contract for 1 or 2 years. New & better phone deals are coming onto the market every day and if you have the ability to leave at any time then this forces the phone company to ensure that your bills are competitively priced and you're not over-charged.

8. Sometimes it's cheaper to make a short call from your mobile than it is to send a large number of text messages.

9. Find a phone plan that allows you to make cheaper calls to a list of nominated numbers.

10. If you make lots of overseas calls – consider using your computer to make them. PC to PC calls are often free, and the PC to phone calls are also often cheaper.

11. Eliminate services you don't need – why pay for Voicemail, Call waiting or Caller ID if you don't use them?

12. Use the phone book instead of calling information and paying for a simple phone number.

13. Use your phone's redial function instead of opting for automatic redialing and callback services.

14. When calling a business or company, always look for a toll-free 1-800 number instead of dialing direct.

15. Investigate phone plans that offer free phones or free minutes.

16. Opt for minute plans that either roll over into the next month or that does not force you to pay for more time than you will use.

17. Enquire about low income price breaks for qualifying households. (This typically applies only to land lines.)

18. Avoid the temptations of text messaging competitions, downloading ring tones, and other extras that heavily increase a phone bill.

19. Choose a family calling plan that offers reduced rates to specific individuals or regions (note that the best deals may require both parties to sign up for the plan).

20. Toll-free calls aren't free when you make them from a mobile phone; so save your 1-800 calls for times when you have access to a landline.

21. If you only use your mobile phone for occasional calls, a prepaid plan may be the cheapest service option for you. Shop around and you could spend as little as $20 every three months.

New Plans

In the Garden

1. Plan and prepare your garden. Doing this will ensure you don't waste money on impulse purchases.

2. Buy seeds or seedlings rather than potted plants, it's less expensive.

3. Look for healthy root systems and foliage when buying plants to ensure the success rate is high.

4. Buy plants that are suitable for the environment where you wish to plant them.

5. Don't hire a gardening service. Mowing, trimming and fertilizing are simple tasks.

6. Shop at small local nurseries, where the plants are healthier and they have competitive prices.

7. Purchase your plants at the beginning of the plant's growing season.

8. Native plants and ground covers are very cost effective.

9. Buy plants that you can lift, divide and re-plant – such as perennials and succulents.

10. Take advantage of free plant offers from local councils or gifts of plants for Christmas.

11. Get plants established well before extreme weather hits.

12. Recycle old egg cartons as 'seed-starters'. The cardboard type cartons can be planted with the seedling intact as they will break down in the soil.

13. Swap cuttings from your garden with other gardeners. This is the most inexpensive way to get new plants. Most gardeners are more than willing to share.

14. Plant your seeds and seedlings in containers you find around your home. Be inventive! Old crockery and dishes make great homes for new plants.

15. Check with local dairy or horse farms. They may offer free manure, especially if you load it yourself.

16. Collect your rainwater. Tanks may be expensive but rainwater can also be piped into fishponds and pools.

17. Rocks make great borders, broken tiles can be used to make mosaic stepping stones.

18. An old pair of work boots with laces will make two great plant pots. Don't forget to drill holes in the bottom for drainage.

19. Fill an old tyre with soil and cactus plants to make a small cost effective cactus garden.

20. Fill an old disused plastic or metal watering can with soil and flowers.

21. Dustbins and compost bags with holes are great for growing potatoes.

22. Buying plants in bulk can be a cheaper alternative as the price can usually be negotiated.

23. Plants that easily multiply are a great way to save dollars on your landscaping budget.

24. Making your own compost will help cut costs of mulch and fertiliser.

25. Compost your garden leftovers as well as your fruit and vegetable scraps from the kitchen. Don't forget that used coffee grounds are great for composting, as are grass clippings and dead leaves.

26. Fallen leaves are also a cheap form of mulch. All it costs is a little time spent in raking.

27. Timeshare your tools. Chip in with your neighbours to buy items you don't need that often, like an aerator or lawnmower, and take turns storing and using the items.

28. Buy plants out of season and keep them ready for planting.

29. Line your planters with newspaper before you add soil. It helps retain water and keeps the soil temperature more constant, thus keeping the plants healthier and saving water. (And watering time!)

30. Scrap wood can yield many projects in the garden, from birdhouses to garden fencing. Your limit is your imagination.

31. An old tree stump can be beautiful with a flowering vine growing over it.

32. Chunks of recycled concrete can make a wonderful retaining wall or garden border.

33. Visit yards where recycled building materials are cheaper to buy.

34. Use old pantyhose as tiebacks for your climbing plants. Cut them into strips and use to tie them to their supports. The hose is soft so as to not damage the plant, and quickly disappears behind the foliage.

35. When you dig up soil for a new garden bed or project, save all the rocks you find along the way in a pile. Later they can be used as edging.

36. Gravel can be used for a patio instead of pavers. It's a cheaper alternative.

37. Making your own weed killer is as simple as buying some distilled vinegar and spraying it on the offending weeds at full strength.

38. Consider whether a different ground cover may be more economical than mulch. (Mulch needs to be replaced and topped up constantly.)

39. Anything that can hold soil can become a planter. An old cracked chimera, a rusted wheelbarrow, or a pretty basket lined with plastic.

40. Irrigate your plants by using the 'drip' method. This not only saves water but also saves water being wasted.

41. To rid your lawn of bindii use a solution of two tablespoons iron sulphate to four litres of water. Spray liberally. The weeds will die and your lawn should start to look lush and green, growing over the bare patch left by the dead bindii. Be sure to wear gloves and old clothes as iron sulphate will stain anything it comes in contact with.

42. Use paint (it's cheap!) to create an interesting fence or wall.

43. Slugs and snails can destroy a garden overnight if the gardener isn't vigilant. A cost-effective solution to this problem is newspaper. Simply shred newspaper and spread around the base of your plants. Then just dampen it slightly and sprinkle with bicarbonate of soda. Snails love damp newspaper while the bicarb acts as a poison to them.

44. Arrange a plant exchange or seed swap party and invite all of your green thumbed pals. Have everybody bring samples from their gardens and trade.

45. For your vegie garden – only spend money on fruits or vegetables your whole family will definitely use. Staggered planting will ensure you have produce for the whole season.

46. Unless you're a professional gardener, there's no need to get too fancy with gardening tools. A spade/shovel, spading fork, hoe and garden shears can go a long way in a budget conscious garden.

47. Arrange with your friends to buy seeds in bulk. The seeds will be cheaper and you can split them among yourselves when they arrive.

48. There's no need to splash out on expensive gardening manuals – there are many places to get good advice for nothing. Your local library and the internet are good places to start

49. Keep your eye out for secondhand garden tools and furniture. You'll be surprised how many are available online and at garage sales.

50. If it all gets too much – concrete can be the solution for all your gardening problems!

Families

Babies
Kids Birthday Parties
Back to School

Planning

Babies

1. Young babies have very simple needs. They need warmth, shelter, milk, cuddles and love so that they can thrive. The rest is just window dressing. Remembering this will help your budget.

2. If you or your spouse is considering leaving the workforce to stay home with a baby, try to live on a single salary throughout the pregnancy.

3. Only shop for baby stuff when there is a sale, most stores generally have a sale every month or so.

4. Many manufacturers give hospitals samples, coupons, and freebies for new parents. Before you come home, ask the nurses or hospital staff if they have any available.

5. Instead of buying bassinette sheets, use flannelette pillowcases and put them over the bassinette mattress. They don't look any different once tucked under the mattress.

6. Instead of a cot consider using a portable one until the baby grows bigger. But take care that it is suitable for your circumstances. For the sheets, cut up single flannelette sheets. Again, when tucked in they don't look any different to bought sheets.

7. Look on eBay for the pram that you'd like as there are many for sale.

8. If you have some unused material and old cushions lying around, make your own breast feeding pillow. You can find a pattern online.

9. Leftover material can cover an old cane basket to hold all of baby's bits and pieces.

10. Use soft washcloths instead of commercial baby wipes. Dampen with a solution of water mixed with a tiny drop of baby shampoo.

11. Cloth wipes are gentler on baby's bottom and can be tossed in the laundry along with the cloth nappies.

12. Join a toy library and borrow the larger play items.

13. Knit little squares with different colours; sew them together then pack with cushion stuffing to make little balls for baby to play with.

14. Download a baby beanie pattern from the internet and make beanies by hand.

15. Instead of buying a nappy bag use an old laptop shoulder bag. It's the same size as most nappy bags.

16. Ask family members to look at their old baby stuff to see if there is anything you can use for your baby instead of buying it.

17. Breast-feed your baby if you're able. It's healthy for you and your baby and will save you money on the cost of formula.

18. Why spend lots of money on commercial jars of baby food when healthier, fresher, homemade purees are easy to make by using a steamer and a blender?

19. Making homemade baby food from ingredients such as fresh bananas, apples, squash, sweet potato, peaches, plums and carrots costs only a few cents per gram as compared to commercial baby foods, which cost about $0.23 per gram.

20. Hand-me-downs are a fantastic way to save money on a new baby and many mothers are happy to share the wealth. They possibly received hand-me-down baby clothing from relatives or friends also.

21. Saving money on retail purchases is best done at the end of a season. For example, when summer comes to a close and the stores are putting out their autumn items, stock up on summer clothes for baby for the following year. Check your baby's growth chart to estimate what your child's size will be in ten months.

22. Buy and sell baby clothes on eBay – a great place if you really feel the need for 'designer' labels.

23. Opportunity shops are also a great place for quality clothing at lower prices.

24. If you knit - use old jumpers or buy second hand jumpers and pull them apart. Re-winding and re-knitting will save heaps!

25. Your baby really doesn't need shoes until he or she learns to walk. Booties or socks work well to keep your infant's feet warm.

26. Make large batches of pureed/mashed fresh vegetables and then freeze in ice-cube trays. Once frozen, they can be stored in press seal/zip lock bags in the freezer. Use only as much as you need when it's meal time, and you'll always have good food available.

27. Cloth nappies have several uses - put over your shoulder as a 'burping cloth'; they're cheaper than a change mat; and can shade baby's face from the sun. The limit is your imagination.

28. Garage sales are excellent - particularly for the bigger items like prams and cots.

29. Ask family members to buy the clothes or educational toys you really need for Christmas or as birthday presents instead of another unwanted toy.

30. Old towels make fabulous home-sewn baby wipes.

31. Don't overspend on baby toiletries - baby cream, baby powder, baby shampoo. Babies already have beautiful skin, and nobody will ever know if you use the generic brand of these products.

32. Cornflour is excellent for nappy rash and much cheaper than commercial brands.

33. If you are using disposable nappies, buy in bulk when they are on sale!

34. If you can get them – 'seconds' in disposable nappies are a great buy.

35. Generic brand nappies are just as good as well-known brands. Just think about how much money you are flushing away.

36. Reusable breast pads made from cloth are a much cheaper option than the disposable types.

37. Instead of buying expensive maternity bras; strapless bras are an easier option when it's time for feeding baby.

38. If you only need occasional babysitting, trade free babysitting with another parent or group of parents.

39. If you can't find a babysitting group – start one!

40. Instead of a fancy nappy disposal system, just use a lidded garbage bin and sprinkle with baking soda to keep odors down.

41. Don't waste money on expensive 'baby/parenting manuals'. If you have nobody to ask for information, then try the library or the internet.

42. Wipe warmers, fancy rompers, colorful plastic nappy disposal bags, and baby seats and positioners are all great extras to have but they're not really necessary. Stick with the basics and you'll have more money for the important stuff.

43. When you've finished with cloth nappies you can always use them as cleaning cloths.

44. Don't let a good sale on baby formula go to waste. Stock up when you can.

45. Use the powdered variety instead of liquid formulas – it stores longer and you don't waste as much.

46. If your baby doesn't drink a full bottle – make smaller bottles. You can always make a little more when necessary.

47. Join a formula club – some of the well-known brands have online clubs where they offer 'gift certificates' to members.

48. Consider sharing the costs of a bulk purchase with other mothers who are using the same formula.

49. Try generic formula – while most mothers shy away from using this, don't forget that it must also adhere to the same Government health regulations in its production as the well-known brands.

50. Another alternative is to make your own homemade baby formula. The World Health Organization has a recipe for homemade infant formula that is suitable for short-term use.

51. If you have a friend who no longer has a baby and has 'leftover' formula – offer to buy it from them at a reduced price.

52. Ask the grandparents of the baby to also join the 'baby clubs' organized by the formula manufacturers. That way you'll get all the benefits at least twice. (Grandparents also like to have formula on-hand at their place.)

53. Check with your pharmacy – they also have generic brand formula made by the more well-known companies and at much better prices.

Things to Remember

Kids Birthday Parties

1. Keep the guest list to a minimum. Most party supply items, such as plates and napkins, are packaged based on an 8-count or for 8 guests, so bear that in mind to save waste.

2. Try to cook, make and prepare as much food yourself – and don't forget that jelly is a much loved party item!

3. Bake the birthday cake or cupcakes yourself to save cash.

4. The advantage of having cupcakes is that you don't need plates or cake forks - only napkins. Leaving the paper baking cases on the cupcakes will also be helpful for little messy people.

5. Host the party at your home. If your house is too small, make use of a public playground or park.

6. Choose a party timeframe such as mid-morning or afternoon and serve snacks that don't require plates. This alleviates the cost of providing a main meal.

7. Ask an artistic friend or a fun relative to help with activities like face painting or some simple games.

8. Host the party outside and let nature serve as your décor.

9. Start your party with a nature hunt or a simple treasure hunt.

10. When buying party supplies, make sure that you buy reusable ones. If you choose a 'timeless' design, some decorations can last for years and through several birthday parties.

11. Party favours seem to have become a big deal over the years, but you're not really breaking any etiquette rules if you don't give them. Young children probably won't even notice!

12. Buy food in bulk and cut fruits and vegetables yourself rather than buying pre-cut trays from the grocery store.

13. Serve drinks from large containers (jugs or 2 litre bottles) to avoid waste and the large cost of individual cans/serves.

14. Send email invitations or make your own paper invitations using craft supplies you already own.

15. Instead of showering your child with material affection, find more meaningful ways to make them shine on their day.

16. Don't forget that children love colour - so you can't go too far wrong with balloons and streamers in your child's favourite colour as decorations.

17. Have a good children's DVD on hand in case the weather turns sour, or the games run out.

18. If you really must have party favours to take home – make some plain cupcakes that the children can decorate at the party.

19. Get them also to decorate plain paper bags to carry home the cupcake/goodies.

20. If parents are staying, you don't have to provide a gourmet meal for them - some simple dips and savoury biscuits will suffice.

21. Hire a small hall instead of an expensive soft play centre, or during the summer months host a party in your own garden.

22. If you're providing food, make sure you have a budget. Ask family to make some sandwiches and bake your own cake.

23. Party games don't have to cost money - musical chairs, pass the parcel with a few homemade biscuits inside, and treasure hunts using the birthday cake as the hidden treasure.

24. Don't feel pressured into spoiling your child with dozens of gifts. They will be given lots so just one birthday and one Christmas present from you is fine.

25. If you're a guest, explain that you are on a budget and make the card yourself. Offer to take homemade biscuits or make the cake as a gift.

Things to Avoid

Back to School

1. It's best to get the list of school supplies needed on the last day of school before the school year finishes. Don't wait until the first day of school - you'll miss out on the summer sales and lose time shopping and searching for materials on the first day of school.

2. From the requested list of supplies, check what you have left over from last year's supplies. For example, you may have glue sticks and glue bottles left over from last year, so check those off your list.

3. Stick to your list! Don't waste your money buying supplies that look cute or because you think your child might need them. There are some children who show up at kindergarten with geometry sets, staplers and hole punchers. They simply don't need these items yet!

4. It might be best to leave your children at home when shopping for supplies - they seem to want to buy everything in sight and pick the expensive brands!

5. When buying markers, ask yourself if it is better to buy the markers that cost $2 more and will probably last the whole year, or to buy the cheap ones at the discount store that dry out as soon as you look at them?

6. Discount stores are great for 80 per cent of school supplies; the rest you'll need to watch out for at the back-to-school sales.

7. Don't purchase a fancy pencil case that will only hold three pencils and a half an eraser. Instead buy a cosmetic bag (boys can have the solid-colour ones). The case will hold all supplies; it has a sturdier zipper and is available at the same price as the pencil case.

8. Identify your child's belongings - every pencil, crayon and marker. If you don't, they may end up in the collection box at school, and so will your money.

9. Reuse artwork or recycle gift wrap or colour comic pages to cover school exercise books.

10. When you buy supplies at discount stores during their back-to-school sales, stock up on items you'll need right through the year, such as pencils, pens, rulers and paper. Some items could be good for Christmas stocking-fillers.

11. Reuse old vinyl binders. Cover them with pictures from magazines and brush on a clear decoupage sealant (found at hobby and craft stores).

12. Teach your children to take care of their belongings as they use them and to put them away after each use. Getting them into this habit will save you a lot of money throughout the years.

13. You can save some serious dollars on your budget if you buy in bulk. Get together with some of the other parents and set a date to go shopping at a large wholesale discounter. You'll be able to get what you need, below retail prices.

14. Go through your child's wardrobe and see what still fits from last year. Make a list of items that you can reuse this year.

15. Go through your home office supplies and compare it to what your child is going to need for the classroom. Try to use what you already have before going out and buying more.

16. Talk to other parents and friends. They may have an older student and don't mind handing down clothes and school supplies that they no longer need.

17. Buy basics such as t-shirts, socks, underwear, shorts and trousers in multiples when they are on sale. Buying out of season saves you the most money, but make sure to calculate the right size for the proper season when buying ahead for fast growing children.

18. For younger children, buy pants with adjustable waistbands. Buy them long and cuff them; as your child grows, let out the waistband bit by bit.

19. Purchase clothes made from durable materials that are easy to wash and dry. That way you can buy less and wash the items often.

20. If you can sew, take a piece of material that is your child's favourite colour and make a pencil case, complete with their name stitched on it. Or even better, get them to do it themselves.

21. Buy used books - your school probably has a used book store or website.

22. See if your friends' children are taking the class, or have taken it, so that you may be able to use their books.

23. If buying electronics - shop around and buy where you can get student discounts.

24. Look for student fares/passes for transportation.

25. Create a desk pencil holder with an old can and a book and magazine holder from used cereal and detergent boxes. Be creative and be on the lookout for how you can make your own supplies from basic household items.

26. Don't spend money on brand new plastic for textbook covers. Save money and be creative by using old gift wrapping paper, newspaper, or plain brown grocery bags

which the kids can draw on and decorate after the book is covered.

27. If your school has no uniform - have your children pick out 2 or 3 of their favourite colours at the start of the school year. Purchase clothes only in those chosen colours in addition to neutrals so that they have a true mix-and-match wardrobe. This makes getting ready in the morning faster and easier, and it maximizes their wardrobes by giving them more possible outfits.

28. Don't let your child wear their school uniform after school. Changing into 'play' clothes will help to preserve the life of the uniform. School uniforms are expensive to replace.

29. Have a moneybox or a jar on top of the fridge for all your loose change – this comes in very handy for cheaper excursions or when your child needs some small change for unplanned school activities.

30. Turn unused pillow cases into Library Bags. Use permanent markers to label them.

School List

Celebrations

Planning
Gifts
Food
Drinks
Decorations
Easter

Planning

1. Ask yourself this – are you planning to be a part of the 'money meltdown' at Christmas or do you have a real plan in place to avoid the 'cash carnage'?

2. It's time to stop making excuses and take some action. Get your finances sorted out - before the end of the year celebrations!

3. Order a copy of "1001 Budget Tips" as a present to yourself.

4. Make a list of everybody that you need to buy a gift for and stick to the list!

5. Work out how much you can comfortably afford to spend on each gift, and do not overspend.

6. At Christmas, consider sending cards instead of presents and then get them written and posted early.

7. Don't try to do it all on your own - get help!

8. Families can get a bit crazy during the Christmas period and sometimes it's hard to keep everything in perspective. A level head and a good sense of humour for both preparation and parties are essential to keep your budget under control.

9. Don't forget that the best party memories are about people and events - the size and cost of the gifts are insignificant.

10. Early preparation for your celebrations will help save the last-minute rush; which always costs you more in the long run.

Gifts

1.   Set a limit for each person, and stick to it!

2.   At Christmas time, consider a Kris Kringle (Secret Santa) for large family gift-giving events; where everyone draws a name out of a hat and buys a present only for that person. (You're not the only one on a budget.)

3.   Give vouchers – lawn mowing; painting; baby-sitting; house cleaning etc. Nowadays people are time poor, not possession poor.

4.   Buy a copy of "*1001 Budget Tips*" as a great gift for somebody!

5.   Choose a theme for your gifts – calendars, books, chocolates, homemade treats, socks, pens, glasses, pillows, etc.

6.   Spending time with loved ones is the best gift of all. Consider a family day pass to the zoo or a theme park. Movie tickets for a family outing will also be appreciated.

7. Make your own gifts. If you enjoy crafts, art or cookery, put your talents to good use and give personal, handmade gifts that will be treasured.

8. Discuss gift giving with your friends. You might be able to mutually agree not to give gifts during the year, or perhaps agree to only buy something small for times when gifts are appropriate.

9. Rather than buying individual presents, just purchase one per couple, or per family. This is a more cost effective way for gift giving.

10. At the beginning of every year start collecting free samples offered online and offline. By the time Christmas arrives, you will have enough stuff for stockings and treat bags without spending any money. There are lots of things you can find for free!

Food

1.   Plan your menu in advance and also use a shopping list.

2.   Compare prices before heading out to purchase your party food. (Use advertising mail for this.)

3.   Don't leave everything to the last minute.

4.   Share the cooking – ask guests to participate by contributing a part of the menu. Don't forget that there are other people who would love to share their 'family favourite'.

5.   Store brands are great for side dishes and salads etc. - nobody will even realise!

6.   If you are cooking lunch at home, delegate tasks. You don't need to do everything yourself!

7.   Consider keeping it simple - you could always arrange for a 'buffet' meal, where everybody brings a platter.

8. Buy as many non-perishable food items as you can in advance - supermarkets are generally extremely busy on the days before major public holidays/celebrations.

9. If you want particular food items (such as turkeys) order them from your supermarket early to avoid disappointment.

10. Book well in advance if you plan to have your celebration at a restaurant. Popular restaurants can book out early and late decisions can cost you more - don't wait until the last minute.

Drinks

1. A lot of money is spent on alcohol for celebrations. Try serving guests a festive glass of punch – you can even stretch out servings with apple juice.

2. Punch goes a long way and is less expensive (alcoholic or non-alcoholic).

3. Use lots of ice – this also helps make drinks last longer when the weather is hot.

4. Rather than hosting a cocktail party – have a coffee and dessert party instead. Set up a coffee bar and have an assortment of cakes and other decadent treats.

5. Serve non-alcoholic cocktails. These are made from bright coloured cordials, lemonade, fruit juices and lots of shaved ice.

6. Check out the 'end-of-bin' sales in your local liquor shop. There are heaps of great wines to be found at fabulous prices.

7. If you're having a Brunch or Lunch party – stretch out the champagne with fruit juices, or even soda water. Your guests will appreciate not feeling too tipsy so early in the day.

8. Serve white wines with soda water or lemonade for a refreshing change.

9. Buy inexpensive glasses and paint each guests name on the side, or attach a tag with each name to a glass stem. As a gift for everyone in attendance, this also helps with not having heaps of glasses to wash. (Each guest takes their gift-glass home.)

10. Have large water jugs of icy water available at all times. This helps to keep guests a little more sober and safe.

Decorations

1. Wrap gifts in bright and glossy junk mail - it all ends up in the same place in the end!

2. Make your own gift cards from leftover last year's cards or scraps of wrapping paper.

3. Give an extra gift by wrapping small gifts in hankies or cloth napkins.

4. Don't over-spend on decorations. Recycle the ones from last year or just add one or two new pieces.

5. Save money on a Christmas tree by decorating one in the garden with lights instead.

6. Make your own homemade decorations, or pick up beautiful vintage bargains at car boot sales or in charity shops.

7. Use children's art-work, they make great decorations too!

8. If you must have Christmas lights all over the place – get solar-powered ones and at least cut down on your electricity usage.

9. Buy inexpensive candles and decorate them yourself with a Christmas theme. Use tinsel, glitter and ribbons

to decorate them and save money, instead of buying pre-packaged Christmas ones.

10. Use the cards that you receive, as part of your decorations. Clipped to a long piece of ribbon, or strung across the room – they make a cheerful and inexpensive feature.

Easter

1. Mini chocolate eggs or cheap bags of chocolate eggs can be shared out amongst several children.

2. Any box can be decorated with cut-out flower pictures, old saved bits of ribbon etc. and can be filled with small Easter treats.

3. Consider buying multi-purpose containers instead of the traditional Easter baskets - such as sand buckets, flower pots, storage containers, etc. This way you will be giving the Easter basket recipient an extra gift.

4. Home-made cookies can be cut into bunny feet shapes and put into gift boxes.

5. Print off Easter pictures for colouring in. Colouring pens can be added and these make great alternative gifts for children.

6. Consider making homemade chocolate, chocolate suckers, bunnies, and so on.

7. Kits with candy moulds can be obtained at your local craft or department store. Not only will the cost of the chocolate be cheaper per kilo to make them, you will be able to use the kits for many years to come.

8. Do some research on how Easter is celebrated in other cultures. Turn your celebration into a learning experience by enjoying traditional Easter foods and activities from another country.

9. Rather than having an elaborate meal with all the trimmings, consider serving a modest meal. Donate the extra money you would have spent to an organisation that feeds the hungry.

10. Have an egg hunt in a new location. Hide the eggs at a new location such as the beach or a park.

11. Rather than just giving the kids large chocolate eggs, give them an original Easter basket full of things to do and eat during the Easter holidays.

Weddings

Outfits
Beauty Hints
The Ceremony
Flowers
The Reception
Cake
Photography
The Honeymoon

Brides Wish List

Outfits

1. It's critical that you remember that you will probably only wear these clothes once. Ask your attendants to contribute financially to the clothes they will wear (after all they do get to keep them) or perhaps pick a themed wedding - fancy costumes are much cheaper than wedding attire.

2. Family heirlooms; dresses, hats and veils, can be brought out from the closet to make special memories and keep the costs down.

3. A smaller bridal party will also mean a smaller bill for the wedding outfits.

4. Your mother or another relative or friend may have a dress that you could borrow.

5. Got your heart set on designer couture? Save up to 30% by simply changing the fabric. For example; a wedding dress made of poly satin will cost far less than silk satin and no-one will even notice.

6. If you're handy with a sewing machine then making the dress yourself could get your dream design at half the cost.

7. If you can't sew then buy a dress pattern and material and find a dressmaker.

8. Most of the big bridal shops have huge sales once a year, make sure you attend.

9. If you wear a small dress size, many designers have a 'sample-sale' once a year. This could be a great opportunity to get a one-off design at a great price.

10. Find the factory outlet of your favourite designer. The prices will be less expensive than the retail outlet.

11. Goodwill and secondhand shops often have pre-loved wedding dresses for sale at varying prices, but much cheaper than elsewhere. You can always use the dress just as the basis for your own additions to create your ideal gown.

12. Online auction sites also have pre-loved dresses for little money and that have only been worn once.

13. Bridal gown cleaning is expensive. When purchasing a pre-loved item, don't pick the one that has a dirty hem or needs cleaning.

14. Hire rather than buy your dresses.

15. Bridal Hire shops sometimes sell off surplus gowns so this may be a good way to get a bargain.

16. If you really don't want to give back your hired dress after the day, then consider buying an ex-rental gown.

17. Bridesmaids' gowns can be bought from evening-wear boutiques. This can shave many dollars off the total bill and will also give a wider choice in styles and colours.

18. Bridesmaids' dresses can also be made if you're heading to a dressmaker or doing it yourself.

19. If your wedding is semi-formal; get the groom to wear a nice suit that he already owns.

20. Encourage all the groomsmen to hire from the same supplier and, in many cases, they will include the groom's tux for free.

21. Shop for wedding rings at wholesalers.

Wedding Jokes

Beauty Hints

1. Do your own hair and makeup.

2. Try to hire one person or company that does both hair and make-up.

3. It's not necessary to purchase all new cosmetics for your wedding. Take your make-up bag to your local beauty counter and ask them to help you create a look with what you already have.

4. Head to your favourite make-up counter in the shopping mall and get a complimentary make-up application. Buy the lipstick so that you'll be able to touch up your lips when needed.

5. Only the bride needs a trial. (For hair and make-up.)

6. Don't waste money on expensive teeth whitening. Dab a little bicarbonate of soda onto your toothbrush and brush your teeth as usual, every day for a week before the wedding.

7. If hair accessories are going to be put in anyone's hair, make sure you buy them yourself. If you leave this up to the hair stylist it'll cost more.

8. Don't risk your wedding day as the first time for a spray tan application. The wrong colour or technique could leave you looking less than perfect. Bronzing pearls or powder will give you an all-over glow.

9. Consider approaching a hairdressing and/or beauty college and offering your wedding as a project. The costs will be minimal and all work is supervised.

10. Remember – the one you are marrying loves you, warts and all. If they were looking for total perfection they'd still be looking.

The Ceremony

1. Focus on what you want rather than what everybody seems to tell you that you should have. All those extras cost dollars.

2. If you get married in a garden, you won't have to decorate it. The flowers are already there!

3. Having a smaller number of attendants is not only easier to manage, but more cost effective.

4. Borrow a friend's car rather than stretching out in a limousine.

5. Don't be afraid to use transport with a difference!

6. If you have a large wedding party then hiring a mini bus may work out a better option.

7. Consider getting married on any day other than a Saturday. You'll be surprised at how much this will cut the costs of everything.

8. Lots of couples get married in springtime. Deciding on a winter wedding will save you heaps!

9. Having your ceremony and reception in the same venue will help to keep costs down.

10. When choosing your wedding invitation, select one that will only require one postage stamp.

11. It is important that your wedding invitations are special; however there is no need to go overboard as your guests will remember your ceremony and wedding reception more than the invitation.

12. Keep invitations simple. Top-quality paper, decorative envelope linings, multiple enclosures and custom-coloured inks all add to the price.

13. To make your invitations more personal and less expensive, do them yourself. There are a number of paper stores and websites available where you can find original ideas and ways to make your own invitations.

14. Order a plain invitation from a company and decorate it yourself. All you need is a hole-puncher and some ribbon and/or parchment paper.

15. Common sense tip - the least amount of people providing a service, the cheaper everything will be.

Flowers

1. You don't have to spend a lot of money in order to have beautiful flowers for your wedding. All you need to do is plan carefully, order well in advance and not be too fussy by wanting flowers that are out of season.

2. Order bouquets without saying it's for a wedding and you'll keep the costs down. You can add the wedding ribbons etc. at home (more cheaply than a florist can).

3. Contact a local floral design school and hire them to provide your flowers.

4. Using beautifully toned foliage for a lot of your displays, maybe with just a few accent flowers, can be magnificent. These can easily be obtained from trees and bushes of friends and family for no cost.

5. Unless you plan on keeping your bouquet on display in your home, don't bother with a duplicate to toss.

6.	Instead of tossing your whole bouquet, just pick one flower to throw. We all know what condition the bride's bouquet becomes after a horde of women start clawing at it.

7.	Having smaller bouquets will mean having a smaller florist bill.

8.	Choosing flowers that are in season will keep your costs lower.

9.	Silk flowers save you a lot of money and they're already preserved. The bride can have fresh flowers, but there really isn't any need for everyone else to have them.

10.	When decorating the church or reception venue consider using silk flowers.

11.	Buy flowers at wholesale prices from the local market for your decoration needs.

12.	Check with your florist or garden centre to see if you can rent plants to decorate the church or venue.

The Reception

1. The wedding reception venue is perhaps one of the biggest expenses. Before you start looking for a suitable place, you need to decide what sort of party you really want. Do you want a traditional formal event with a sit-down dinner, followed by dancing? (There's another expense to provide the music.) Or perhaps you would prefer a quieter more intimate affair for a few people.

2. If you have a small budget consider a brunch reception as the food cost is usually a lot less and your guests will usually not drink as much.

3. Always ask the caterer for the low-cost menu plans first. They have plenty of great ideas on how to cut back the cost of the food, whilst still making it look and taste sensational.

4. You don't need to have a 'rehearsal dinner'. Seriously, you'll all be getting together for eats and drinks on the day of the wedding anyway. Cut the expense!

5. If you must have a rehearsal dinner, consider a backyard barbeque or picnic in the park to keep the costs down.

6. Check with your local groups such as the Country Women's Association, church groups, and other service organisations. They may do catering, and charge a smaller price than commercial businesses. You will also see the benefit of your money going to help others, in any profit they make.

7. Have you considered holding the reception in your yard? It's not as difficult as you might think. Look for an inexpensive catering company and perhaps a cheap marquee.

8. Hire a caterer that supplies everything you need, plates, glassware, table cloths, etc.

9. If you're having a wedding with 75 guests or under, consider having your reception at your favourite restaurant. You will already know the staff and how good the food is.

10. Stick to serving food that everyone is familiar with. Fancy food is expensive.

11. Having no children at the wedding reception can also greatly reduce the numbers and save you a fortune.

12. Choosing your venue and your catering should be done at the same time. Allow extra money for emergencies that might crop up - such as an increase in food prices etc.

13. If you're doing your own catering, a buffet style meal can sometimes be more expensive than a sit down menu. That's because everybody has a different idea on portions.

14. Finger food stand-up affairs can be cheaper than a full-blown three-course meal. Not only do they usually require less time which saves hiring costs and food costs, but you won't be able to fit in as many speeches.

15. Consider a stand-up winetasting tapas style reception. Guests get to sample a little of everything and your wallet doesn't thin out as quickly.

16. Think about a buffet menu from a different culture. Thai cuisine, Indian food or Japanese meals are generally not budget busters.

17. A vegetarian menu or even a vegetarian entrée will help to keep costs down.

18. Many couples divide the catering bill into two – food and beverages. This can be a reasonable way of sharing the costs between families.

19. Cutting the time frame of the reception from 5 hours to 3 hours will cut big dollars off your bill.

20. If you're paying for all the drinks yourself then it's a much more cost effective plan to stick to some basic drinks (beer, wine, soft drink) and let the guests know that if they desire anything else, they will have to pay for it themselves.

21. If money is really tight – perhaps ask your guests to pay for their own meal instead of bringing a gift.

22. Hire a DJ rather than a band.

23. Find an up-and-coming band that would jump at the chance to be a part of your day.

24. Make a playlist of all your favourite songs on your iPod and have it playing softly throughout the reception. Ramp up the volume when you're ready to dance.

Cake

1. These days there is no hard and fast rule about the wedding cake. Traditionally, a wedding cake was a fruit cake decorated with almond icing and a 'wedding couple' figurine on top. It was cut into small pieces, placed into gift bags and given to all the guests as a small gift. Nowadays, brides choose all sorts of different types of cake as their wedding cake and once again the decision is only limited by your budget.

2. Bake the cake yourself and have it professionally decorated.

3. Ask a cake decorating class if they'd like to take on your wedding cake as a project. You pay for the materials of course.

4. It can be an enormous help to your budget if you combine your wedding cake as part of your meal and perhaps use it as dessert.

5. Consider buying the cake undecorated and having a flower arrangement made for the top of the cake. This looks fantastic and the price difference is huge.

6. Another suggestion is to just have an 8" cake as a centrepiece and surround it by cupcakes. Positioned on a tiered cake plate – the whole arrangement can look stunning.

7. Each guest then receives a cupcake as either a memento or dessert and the larger one can be kept for another time. It's an inexpensive way to celebrate with a cake.

8. A mud cake or a sponge cake costs less than a traditional fruit cake.

9. Purchase an un-iced 'slab cake' from the bakery and cut it into any shape you want. Have it iced in accordance with your budget.

10. A frosted wedding cake can be a budget alternative to the traditional almond icing.

11. Try a cheesecake option with different sized cheesecakes on stands. Once cut, serve with various flavoured sauces as a deliciously memorable dessert.

12. Who says you have to have cake? A 'Bombe Alaska' or Pavlova can make a stunning and delicious alternative that can also be eaten as dessert.

Photography

1. Approach a photography school and ask if their students might like to use your wedding as a project. Offer to purchase their best shots.

2. Buy a few disposable cameras and ask several guests to take the pictures for you. Generally, the developing is included in the price of the camera.

3. Cut the photographers' hours by eliminating the pre-wedding shots.

4. If you decide on a professional, decide beforehand how much you have to spend and what you need. Be very clear in conveying your wishes, and don't be talked into a more expensive package.

5. If you know somebody that takes good photos with a digital camera, ask them to photograph your day. Offer them a meal in return for the digital file.

6. The full length framed photo is gorgeous for the first few years, but you'll need a very large wall to hang it on and it'll probably cost you the same as a mortgage payment.

7. Hire a photographer who will give you your digital high resolution files. Then you can make as many copies of pictures from your wedding day as you want without having to order them from the photographer.

8. If you choose a photographer that doesn't give you your files, always find out how long they keep your files for and ask if you can have them when they are ready to discard them. Most photographers in general don't keep digital photos past 3 years. Be prepared that some photographers may still charge a fee for providing your files.

9. Don't just look at the photo packages or wedding day shoot costs, ask how much their enlargements and albums are.

10. If you really do want to have a film of the day then perhaps contact your local university or TAFE to hire a promising student to film your wedding. Some of these students have the latest knowledge and access to top equipment.

The Honeymoon

1. Your wedding budget should also include your honeymoon. Work out which priorities are most important and allocate the money accordingly. You may be able to spend less on some aspects of your wedding so that more of your budget can go towards your honeymoon.

2. Don't book the 'honeymoon suite'. Generally the only difference between that and any other nice room is the gift of a bottle of bubbly and chocolates.

3. Special promotions and standby deals can make your honeymoon costs much easier on the wallet.

4. You don't have to go away immediately after the wedding. Stay in a nice hotel for the wedding night and then save for a huge holiday to celebrate your 1st wedding anniversary.

5. Deferring your honeymoon to take advantage of low-season holiday rates will cost you less.

6. Save money on airfares and upgrade to a nicer resort/hotel/room within driving distance. You'll possibly be able to stay a little longer also.

7. Consider a B & B – most have deluxe amenities and you'll find plenty with romantic settings or nooks.

Packing List

Helping

the

Environment

Cooling
Heating
Electricity
Refrigeration
Saving the Planet

Hints

Cooling

1. Invest in ceiling fans if you do not already have them.

2. Turn up the thermostat on your air-conditioner. The colder you try to make your house/room/office – the more energy you use, thus making your electricity bill higher.

3. If it's possible, place your air-conditioning unit in a cool or shaded area. If the unit is in direct sunlight, it uses more energy to cool your house.

4. Awnings and sun screens can reduce the temperature by around 20%. They protect your windows from direct sunlight, which greatly helps reduce heat.

5. Planting trees around your home will keep it shaded and cooler.

6. Avoid landscaping with lots of unshaded rock, cement, or asphalt on the southern or western sides. It increases the temperature around the house and radiates heat to the house after the sun has set.

7. Replace incandescent globes with compact fluorescents; they produce the same light but use 20% less energy and heat. Consider using LED's which are even more efficient.

8. Add insulation around air-conditioning ducts when they are located in unconditioned spaces such as attics, ceiling

spaces, and garages; do the same for whole house fans that are open to the exterior or to the attic.

9. Caulking and weather stripping around doors and windows will keep cool air in during the summer.

10. Check to see that your fireplace damper is tightly closed. This stops cool air escaping, and hot air from coming inside.

Heating

1. Only heat the space that you are in. Central heating is great, but if your family only use one or two rooms then you are throwing away vast amounts of energy and money to heat the entire house.

2. Heat just 'yourself'. Hot water bottles, microwaveable rice pillows and chenille blankets are all things that will keep you warm whilst you're sitting or sleeping.

3. Make sure your home is insulated!

4. Draw your curtains as soon as it gets dark – windows lose more heat than walls and covering them with your curtains will ensure that you keep as much of your heat inside as possible. If you don't have curtains, think about getting some.

5. Hang a blanket or curtains over the doors. This will also help to keep the warmth in the room. Glass doors allow a lot of heat to escape, just like windows.

6. Get a nice woolly hat. A lot of body heat is expelled through the top of the head, so covering up will keep the heat in!

7. Putting a blanket under the bottom sheet (between the sheet and the mattress) really makes a difference to the warmth in bed. Try it and see for yourself.

8. If you feel cold most when you get out of bed - have a hot shower to warm you up.

9. Hot drinks will help to keep you warm inside, as will a hot meal for breakfast (porridge is inexpensive) and a hot meal at night.

10. Warm the house up to a temperature where you can be warm in a sweater. Your house doesn't need to be hot enough for shorts. Remember - it's winter, so dress accordingly.

11. Stop up all the gaps with draught excluders. If you don't have store bought ones use old folded curtains or old folded towels. They stop the air flow just the same.

12. Keep the windows and doors tightly closed, and make as few trips in and out of the home as possible. This will mean that it takes less energy to heat your home, resulting in a smaller energy bill.

13. Get physical. Exercise! Jump up and down, or run in one spot. Break into a sweat. This will bring up your body temperature, and you may find yourself needing to cool down.

14. Most overhead fans have two settings. They can spin one way, blowing cold air down; or the opposite direction, pushing cold air up. In the winter, change the setting of your fan so that it pushes cold air up - keeping the warm air down below, where you are.

15. Going for a brisk walk before bedtime will get your blood circulating and this will keep you warm enough to undress and get ready for bed.

16. Thermal underwear is excellent! It might look a bit daggy, but nobody sees it and it's better to be warm and look happy than feel cold and look miserable.

17. Put hot water bottles into your bed an hour before you go to bed. Warm your nightclothes before the heater so that you can put warm night clothes on.

Comparison Costs

Electricity

1. Turn off your television, video, hifi, PlayStation, computer and other entertainment devices when they are not being used.

2. Do not leave your television etc. in standby mode. Devices can use up to 90% as much power in standby mode as when they are on, so it's waste of energy when a device is left constantly on standby. Consider purchasing a power saving device which automatically cuts power to appliances when they go into standby mode.

3. Replace your inefficient incandescent light globes with energy efficient Compact Fluorescent Lamps. Replace halogen spotlights with much more efficient and longer lasting LED spotlights.

4. Hang your clothes out to dry rather than using an electric tumble dryer. Ideally use a spin dryer before using the tumble dryer.

5. Cook many items at the same time when your electric oven is already hot. You have more than rack in your oven, use 2 or more at the same time.

6. Use a microwave to reheat food or to cook small portions. Although a microwave uses a lot of power, it does so over a very short time and so saves energy overall.

7. Turn down your heating system thermostat. For every degree you lower your heat you can reduce your heating bill by up to

5%. Wear an extra layer of clothing in the house so that you stay warm. Rooms that are rarely used can have their heating turned all the way down or off.

8. Purchase energy efficient white goods (washing machines, tumble dryers, fridges etc.). Although they may cost a little more initially, the cost savings in electricity will cover that many times over.

9. Fold clothes straight out of the tumble dryer while they are still warm to save on ironing.

10. Do not put uncovered liquids into the fridge. Their evaporation will make the fridge have to work harder.

11. If you are cooking small items, use the frying pan.

12. Fan forced ovens reduce cooking costs.

13. To cook vegetables the water doesn't need to be boiling furiously - a gentle simmer is enough.

14. Heat only as much water in an electric kettle as you require for drinks and cooking.

15. Use a convection microwave oven. A small fan inside circulates hot air throughout the oven cutting cooking times by up to 30%.

16. Don't preheat the oven for roasting.

17. Pressure cookers can save up to 25% of power.

18. Don't keep opening the oven door. Every time you do so, your oven loses 20°C of heat.

19. Put lamps in the corner of a room so that the light is reflected off two walls.

20. Turn down the temperature on your washing machine. Heating the water uses the majority of the electricity, so by doing a warm wash instead of a hot wash, big savings are possible.

21. Don't buy a large washing machine if you don't need it. For the occasional big wash an extra cycle or two is cheaper than underutilising a large washer.

22. Suds savers allow you to reuse hot water thus saving your money.

Reminders

Refrigeration

1.   Defrost your fridge or freezer before the ice build-up is 1cm thick.

2.   Make sure the door seals well. If a piece of paper will slide easily between the cabinet and the door, the seal is not good enough.

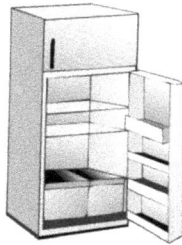

3.   Vacuum clean the condenser coils at the back or underneath your fridge or freezer. Accumulated fluff/dust reduces their efficiency by up to 25%, adding that cost to your electricity bill.

4.   Buy the size of fridge you need - extra capacity uses extra power.

5.   Open the door only when necessary. Don't let your teenager prop on the door whilst deciding what to eat/drink.

6.   If you already have a chest or upright freezer, buy a refrigerator instead of a fridge/freezer combination.

7. Place your fridge away from direct sunlight or any source of heat.

8. Cool cooked food before you put it into the fridge.

9. Keep your fridge full, but not so full that air cannot circulate properly.

10. Defrost frozen food in the fridge since this helps to cool the fridge.

Saving the Planet

1. Where possible whilst wrapping, storing or cleaning - use cloth instead of paper.

2. Use rags for cleaning and polishing, instead of paper towels.

3. Old wash cloths and dish cloths make good dusting cloths.

4. Cut up old bath towels and hand towels to use for polishing silverware and shoes.

5. Use handkerchiefs instead of tissues.

6. Use cloth napkins at the dinner table, instead of paper serviettes.

7. If your table cloth is worn, cut it up and hem the squares to make cloth napkins.

8. Use real dinnerware instead of paper plates and cups.

9. Wrap gifts in handkerchiefs or scarves, as an extra gift for a loved one and the environment.

10. Wrapping your lunch in a slightly dampened napkin will help to keep it fresh.

Notes

Money

Personal Finances
Small Business

Personal Finances

1. Use cash! Paying by cash will make you think twice about breaking a $50 note. It will also make you more aware about where your money is going.

2. Get an empty jar for loose coins. Every time you get home put any coins you may have in your pocket or purse into the jar. It won't make you a millionaire but it all adds up over time.

3. Save for the future. It's a good habit to have – a little often is a good rule of thumb.

4. Credit cards are good! But the golden rule; if you use it, then you must pay it out in full at the end of the month.

5. Keep your insurance policies up to date and relevant. Check them each year at renewal time, to make sure they're still affordable and offering value for money.

6. Pay your credit card bill on time to avoid late fees and interest.

7. Maintain a minimum amount in your bank account to avoid paying fees and fees for being over-drawn.

8. If you are paying high interest charges for credit cards, car loans, personal loans and other debt, you could be wasting lots of money. You may find it better to consolidate all your loans.

9.   Get the best deal for your mortgage - it will be the largest single expense in your budget.

10. Look for bank accounts that pay interest on your money and then use those ones.

11. Make sure you are getting the best deal on all your insurances as well as repairs and maintenance.

12. Shop around to make sure you're not overpaying for your banking - there's a lot of variation in fee structures from bank to bank.

13. Determine your goals, both long term and short term, and calculate how much money you will need to achieve them.

14. Firstly, find out where the money is going now.

15. You can have more for less money, when you learn to be wiser with your money.

16. Consider this - for every $20 you save, you could have one hour off work.

17. Avoid trying to forecast your expenses too far into the future. Doing so can result in inaccurate budgets and overspending.

18. When considering the cost of an item, take into account how long it will last and how many uses you will get out of it. Sometimes the cheaper item won't last as long. Be prepared to save a little longer if that's the case.

19. Check that you don't get overcharged for things.

20. If you have a problem saving, perhaps an automatic deduction from your wages straight into a separate bank account with limited access might help. You can't miss what you don't have.

21. Consider using any wage rises to increase savings. Have them automatically directed to your savings account.

22. Balance your bank account regularly so that you have a good idea of how much money is sitting in your bank account, what deposits and payments have cleared, and any errors that you, or your bank, may have made. It pays to keep in touch with what you have in the bank.

23. Have a regular family spending inventory. This is one way to keep up with where the money is going!

24. When moving house, save loads of time and money by planning ahead. Sell whatever you don't want to take on

eBay, or have a garage sale. The money you make will help to fund your move!

25. Keeping track of your income and expenses can prevent you from overdrawing your account and will also help you track where you money is going.

26. Put yourself on an allowance.

27. If you need a card, have a debit card not a credit card. This allows you to do basically the same things as a credit card, but you can only use the money you have in your account, not run up debt.

28. Never spend a 50 cent coin. Put them into your 'money-jar' and before long you'll have a considerable sum of money.

29. Put away a small amount each month, perhaps $50, to use for Christmas. If you start early enough you could save $550 plus a little interest, by the end of November.

30. Teach your children the value of saving from as young an age as possible. Let them start with their pocket money - saving 10% to start, then moving to investing as the savings grow.

31. Savings habits learnt young, even with pocket money, tend to stick for a lifetime.

32. Make a list of the items in your wallet and have phone numbers handy for lost or stolen credit cards. Replacing items from a lost wallet or purse can be expensive.

33. The easiest and most simple way to save money is simply to use less - of everything.

34. If you don't have the cash, don't buy it.

35. Choose one day a week as a 'no buy day', when you leave your money and credit/debit cards at home.

36. If you need something, see if you can temporarily borrow it from someone rather than buy it. This doesn't mean borrowing, never to give it back!

37. If you use a cheque account, make sure you keep a sufficient amount in it to avoid fees.

38. Make sure you get all the tax refunds etc. that are due to you.

39. Claim any government benefits you are entitled to - child care, family benefits, study benefits, job search allowances.

40. Make use of the 'four day' principle. When you see something you want to buy, wait four days and see if you still want it.

41. Pay your mortgage weekly or fortnightly as interest is calculated daily. By paying it more often you reduce the interest paid overall.

42. Leave your credit card at home; the less temptation, the better.

43. Make an inventory of your contents when you renew your insurance policy. Apply a value against each item and calculate the total insurance value. Update the inventory every time you renew the policy.

44. Consider an 'education savings' account to help off-set future expenses in study and education.

45. Learn how to ask for a raise from your employer.

46. Buy a weekly gift-card for the supermarket and leave your wallet at home when you buy groceries – a sure way of making sure you don't overspend.

47. For every payment you pay late, you are charged a late fee, which can be up to $50 depending on the company. If you are constantly paying these fees then you are going to have trouble balancing your budget. To avoid spending unnecessary money, be sure you make your bill payments in time to avoid these fees.

48. Quit playing the lottery for a month and put the money aside. Calculate how much you have at the end of the month then make an informed decision about your chances of winning versus the money you can put towards real rewards.

49. Pick an amount to have as a minimum in your savings account and make that the 'fail safe' line.

50. Physically go to the bank to take money directly out of your account - you will be more aware of what you are doing.

51. Don't use any ATMs that will charge you a fee.

52. Teaching your kids how to budget and save money is more valuable than you just building up a bank account for them. Make it a family project and that way everyone will feel comfortable discussing money matters.

53. Record your mobile phone IMEI number so that you can inform your carrier if your phone is lost or stolen. The IMEI can be found by pressing *#06#.

54. Find a bank that doesn't charge ATM fees no matter which ATM you use. There are some that do this!

55. Apply for a rewards card from your discount store/supermarket chain and receive the benefit of awards every time you shop at that chain.

56. Record all your expenses that may be tax deductions and keep the receipts for your tax return.

57. Take photographs of valuable items in your home. Also record serial numbers of any electrical equipment. This will help if you ever need to make a claim on your insurance policy.

Savings Plan

Small Business

1. Do your home budget before you start your business budget. Knowing how much you need to earn to cover your household expenses will show you how often you need to work and how much to charge.

2. Once you know how much you need to earn, do a budget for your business using the same method and principles that you used for your household budget.

3. Using second-hand equipment when starting out will save you money that can be spent in other areas of your business.

4. Learn to be frugal with your advertising dollars. There are many low-cost ways to market your business.

5. Don't be afraid to use a 'barter system' with other businesses. This can help to keep costs down for both of you.

6. Look for office stationery and supplies in discount stores and large department stores. You will find that you can purchase generic brands at lower costs than office supplies stores.

7. Don't be afraid to say 'no'. If you don't have the cash for a 'nice-to-have' then do not be 'sold' into borrowing money for it.

8.	Learn the difference between 'advertising' and 'marketing'. You'll be amazed how much you can save.

9.	Leasing equipment is not always the best option – discuss the advantages of purchasing with your accountant.

10.	Cardboard boxes are a cheap alternative for filing and keeping things neat if you don't have the money for fancy storage systems.

11.	Don't get suckered in by the hordes who make it their business to sell you pretty much useless 'tools and techniques'.

12.	Look for those who have made a successful business and analyse why they have been successful.

13.	Try to search out cheaper alternatives and if you can do it yourself have a go.

14.	Don't underestimate the power of social media as a means of getting your product or service out there into the marketplace.

15.	Invest in a good accounting system which will prove invaluable for recording your income/expenditure and for keeping the necessary information for tax etc.

16.	Have a failsafe back-up system for your important data and store it away from your business premises.

17.   Review your communication needs and costs then shop around for the best deals on mobiles, telephone and internet.

18.   Don't just accept the first price offered by a salesperson. Enquire as to what discounts are available and what is required to be eligible for them.

19.   Don't be afraid to shop around for new suppliers if you need to save money for your business.

20.   Dedicate a percentage of your profits every month for outsourcing - so that you can grow at a steady and manageable pace.

21.   Don't spend money on something if you are not going to track the results to see if it worked or not.

22.   Be diligent about keeping tabs on where your clients hear about you so that you will know if you are spending money on marketing/advertising in the right areas.

23.   Send a hand written thank-you note to someone who has sent you some business. Showing gratitude for a business referral is classy and doesn't have to cost a lot of money. It's the simple things that are worth banking on!

24. Keep your personal and home money separate from your business. Keep separate bank accounts and income/expense sheets. Common sense is not always common!

25. Before any problems arise, talk with your company's suppliers. Reaffirm your relationship with them and ask about renegotiating your credit terms if your business should fall on hard times. It is better to have this type of plan set up in advance in case the worst happens.

26. Watch your accounts receivable to be sure your credit customers are not falling behind with their payments. If they get behind then you are also in danger of getting into trouble.

27. If you need to reduce your administrative expenses – do so by cutting them and your office expenses to the bone. Reduce company travel as much as possible. Cut office supplies, expense accounts, lunches out, and long distance telephone costs.

28. Don't try to budget to the last cent. Accurately predicting actual results is not the objective. It's all about giving your business a direction to use.

29. If you try to forecast every little expense, the detail will drive you crazy.

30. Without discipline you will almost always overspend, because there are always good reasons to spend money. They don't always produce more profit for your business.

31. Not all businesses are alike, but there are similarities and all businesses need a budget.

32. Don't choose your suppliers on price alone. If their service is crappy it'll cost you more in the long run.

33. Good prices and good service do go hand in hand – it's the sign of a good business.

34. Before advertising - call your customers to see if there's anything you can do for them. You'll be surprised at the results.

35. Use free marketing when possible. Marketing is about thinking outside the square to attract and engage your audience.

My Business Plan

Making It Work

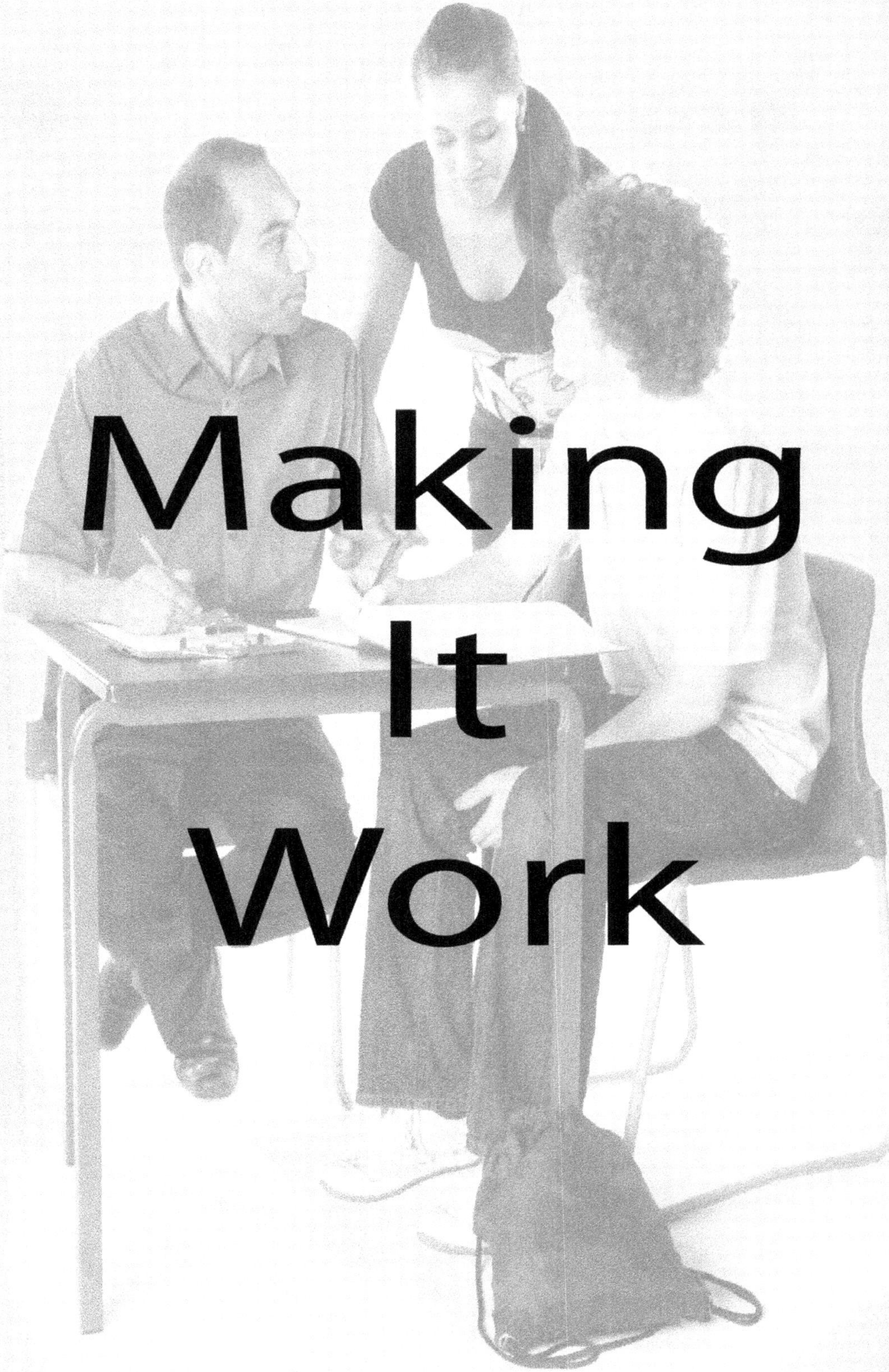

Making it Work

1. Your budget needs to be simple – simple to understand and simple to follow.

2. Your budget should be easy enough to be implemented quickly.

3. If you cannot remember how much money you are able to spend in the supermarket, then your budget is too hard.

4. You should know exactly how much you need to cover your weekly 'must have' expenses.

5. You should be able to work out your budget without the use of a spreadsheet or a complicated formula.

6. Having a budget is not about spending every single cent that you earn.

7. Your budget should reflect a true picture of the values and priorities of your household.

8. Even if you think your budget is ok – it should be reviewed regularly. It's important to keep your budgeting skills sharp.

Things to Do

1.

2.

3.

4.

5.

6.

INDEX

ABOUT THE AUTHOR

Carmel McCartin is an accomplished writer and speaker. Her articles have been published both online and in the print media. This is her second book.

She established the Budget Bitch company in 2007 after two years research whilst working as a personal budget consultant. Carmel has appeared on the Nine Network's *Money Show* as a specialist budgeting reporter. She is a regular commentator on the Prime Network for local and current budgeting issues.

As Australia's #1 *Budget Guru* she has been called "The Chick who takes no crap from anyone" and "the next person to dabble with your wallet".

The tips in this book provide a great start for anyone serious about getting their personal finances in order.

Want to know more?
Need some personalised help?

www.budgetbitch.com.au

www.ingramcontent.com/pod-product-compliance
Lightning Source LLC
Chambersburg PA
CBHW060022210326
41520CB00009B/961